GOOD GOD
FAITH FOR THE REST OF US
DANIEL A. WEINER

CLASSIC DAY
PUBLISHING

Seattle, Washington
Portland, Oregon
Denver, Colorado
Vancouver, B.C.
Scottsdale, Arizona
Minneapolis, Minnesota

Printed in the United States of America

Cover Design: Devlin Donnelly
Text Design: Soundview Design Studio

*Check out www.goodgodforus.com where you will find more information
about this book and special free resources, including a reader's/study guide,
lesson plan for educators and a blog on spirituality, religion and how they
impact politics and popular culture.*

Classic Day Publishing
2925 Fairview Avenue East
Seattle, Washington 98102
877-728-8837
info@classicdaypub.com

It is not good for man to be alone

Genesis 2:18

To Cindy, Julia and Benjamin

For your time and patience

For your love and support

For a bond that strengthens my commitment to others

Contents

Acknowledgements

I AM GRATEFUL TO MANY WHO PROVIDED DIRECT INSIGHT AND INPUT, AND THOSE WHO GAVE ME THE TIME AND SPACE TO WRITE THIS BOOK.

To my wife Cindy, and children, Julia and Benjamin, who sacrificed my scarce and precious free time to allow me to pour myself into this enterprise over the last few years.

To the members of Temple De Hirsch Sinai of Seattle and Bellevue, Washington, for inviting me into their homes and into their hearts, inspiring me to dedicate myself to the Jewish people and Jewish message, and supporting our joint efforts to make our congregation a welcoming, relevant and holy place.

To my Executive Assistant Cathleen Kallmeyer, for her irrepressible humor, indefatigable spirit, and unqualified devotion to our calling.

To Erin Hart and Devlin Donnelly, for their technical expertise and generous offerings of time.

And to Elliott Wolf for believing in my passion and making real my dreams.

Preface

I'M SITTING IN THE SAME STARBUCKS DESCRIBED IN THE FIRST CHAPTER, THOUGH AT A DIFFERENT TIME AND TABLE. Today is a liminal moment for our nation and our world, tritely but aptly labeled "historic." I have just cast my vote in an election which, if the polls hold and the pundits are right, will elect the first African-American president in the nation's two hundred and thirty-two years. Regardless of preference or outcome, the significance of this transitional election and the symbolic power of Barack Obama's candidacy portend change and promise that will forever alter the social and cultural landscape in America.

Some have deemed this, I believe correctly, to be the first election of the 21st century. Despite occurring almost a decade into the new century, the stakes, challenges, and possibilities in this contest authentically reflect the evolving nature of our society. The rising voice and influence of our multi-cultural citizenry, economic pressures emerging from cascading scarcity, the expanding chasm between the haves and have nots in resources, life experience and capacity for empathy, and a global community symbiotically bound to rise or fall together and as One have rendered 2008 the dawn of a new epoch.

Our time is fraught and inspiring. Dangers terrify and dreams empower. It is one of those "foxhole" moments that proverbially belie atheists, filling hearts and minds with elemental faith to assuage existential uncertainty. There is a need for faith that transcends doctrine and dogma, a longing for a path and purpose that girds in the face of fear, guides through the thickets of moral dilemma, and emboldens a closing of the distance between reach and grasp.

The nature of faith and the dynamic tension between personal spirituality, communal need and timeless traditions are other evolving and malleable assumptions in this transitional time. If faith, religion and spirituality are to remain relevant, to have a voice and a vote in the critical discussions and debates that we will face, we must continue to evaluate and assess, modify and amend their principles and practice. Enduring sacred systems have always done so. The calcified and corrupt fill scarcely consulted archives as anthropological oddities. Faith communities that fail to confront changing need and creatively adapt will find an honored but arcane place in the annals of past glory.

These are exciting and anxious times. What we do and what we defer will determine the fate of our children and grandchildren. I am proud to be a part of this unfolding human narrative. And I offer this brief testament as my humble contribution to a conversation that I hope—that I pray—will renew faith for a world in need of the call and power of the spirit.

November 4, 2008
Bellevue, Washington

Talkin' Bout
My Degeneration

IT WAS AN UNUSUAL SCENE, EVEN FOR A STARBUCKS. The ubiquitous café-turned-21st century town square has become a social center for urban neighborhoods and suburban developments. Many cultural observers offer eulogies for the dearly departed community of our imagined past, yet the caffeinated giant has recreated social space for bonding and discussion, four dollar latte not included. My daily visit fixes the cravings of my java jones. But I also seek a bit of the spirit of European café society. I read and study, meet friends, and occasionally talk politics, free from the carcinogenic haze that engulfed the Parisian coffeehouses of the 20s, recently outlawed by the healthy regimen of the West Coast.

Gone with the smoke of filter-less Gitanes is the artistic and intellectual climate that took root in that fertile soil of espresso grounds and strong opinion, loudly stated. Now, one shares the room with Oprah book groups, PTA meetings, interior decorators soft-selling their clients, and any number of toddler play-groups unleashed by weary mothers to raid the straw dispenser and wreak havoc on the French press display. It's a scene that would plague Hieronymous Bosch with nightmares, made more surreal by the soothing tones of a Corrine Bailey Rae compilation piped into the din just below conscious level.

I was hidden in the back corner of the store on just such a day, trying my best to focus on the *New York Times,* embracing this opportunity to test my powers of concen-tration and, zen-like, free myself from the distractions of sibling fights over kung-fu amphibians and house-fraus dishing gossip about television shows depicting more desperate house-fraus dishing gossip. I don't know what caused me to look up at that moment, but I glanced across the room and saw her. Her eyes were as tightly closed as the bun that tied back her hair. She was young and attractive, yet the angst or intensity writ across her face distorted her appearance. She was wearing a white blouse and dark pants, the uniform of the 30-something middle class, yet there was something ancient and wea-ry about her. She clenched the hand of a woman whose back was to me, reaching across the end table that separated the cushy chairs. I tried not to stare, but there was rare beauty in this poignant moment of feeling amidst all the commerce and cackling.

I wondered what she was doing, why she was so troubled, so intent. I got up to leave, seizing a subtle opportunity to take a closer look on my way out. As I passed, her pose and focus unchanged, I noticed a book on her lap. I knew what it was before I'd even fully seen it. The black leather cover and red guilded pages were as identifiable as the phone book. It was one of those classic editions of the Bible used by generations of Protestants. It lacked the verve and hook of more recent versions, with fonts and layouts crafted for surfers, soccer moms, and Nascar dads. But it had a prestige and power beyond its contents. It was a symbol, a talisman passed through the generations, births, deaths, and weddings gently inscribed in its front cover for family posterity.

The book seemed to have a greater impact resting on her lap than opened on a desk. And it revealed something both personal and profound about her and about this moment in our culture. She found solace, created sacred space, carved out a refuge for prayer in the most public and least likely of places and moments. This was more than striking a balance between faith and the world, between the timeless rhythms of religion and the timely trends of the contemporary. She seemed to live in both worlds simultaneously, able to move effortlessly from the coffee klatch to the inner sanctums of the self and of tradition.

More than a straddling between competing worlds, this was an integration of realms that allowed her to revel in both and remain unshackled by either. I wish I had talked to her. Maybe I would have learned about her gifts, or perhaps discovered the more likely projections of my own desires, frustrations, and disappointments. The qualities I saw in her, or what I thought I saw in her, have much to offer this troubled and divided world.

Faith is both healing balm and divisive blade, depending on who uses or abuses its teachings and powers. Many see faith as the only path to human redemption, others as the root cause of all human suffering. The dominant voices in this cultural conversation are inevitably on the extremes, the fanatical fundamentalists and the arch secularists. They provide the best fodder to feed the needy beast of the 24/7 news cycle. But their skewed views, overplayed in the press and exploited by the powerful, confuse and distort the authentic, core messages of

Jewish, Christian, and Muslim faith traditions: the need to love one another, to show compassion for inevitable suffering, to join in supportive community, and to sense a power that transcends the physical, even death.

As our society deteriorates into opposing camps driven by partisan politics and the culture war it has spawned, I'd settle for a better *balance* between private faith and the public square, and leave the *integration* I saw in my Lady Starbucks for the Second or First Coming, depending on who's book you read. We prize our evolved breakthroughs in science to conquer disease, art to push the limits of the creative spirit, and political principles to bring democracy and pluralism to the farthest reaches of the globe. Yet when it comes to matters of faith, values, and the way they play out in the real, modern world beyond the walls of the house of worship, we have quickly crept back to the trials and disputations of the 16th century. The Second Coming is here, not of the Chosen One, but of the seemingly endless conflict between faith and reason, between the Enlightenment and the Established Religious Order. The emotional, psychological, and spiritual insecurities of 400 years ago have resurfaced, with all the dysfunction and destructiveness you might expect when any living thing, let alone a civilization, regresses to a dark, earlier stage in its development.

We are Peter Pans of faith, a spiritually immature global culture that stubbornly refuses to move beyond old views and positions. Past battles between "believers" and "modernists" were never as pronounced as extremists portray them today. But in replaying this imagined conflict upon the contemporary stage, with weapons more destructive and a will to holy war more entrenched, we threaten to realize in our day the hellish visions of conflict, pain, and death that never were, but could be.

Putting the "Fun" in Fundamentalism

The wheels have turned, and it's morning in America for fundamentalists. In a culture that celebrates *X-treme* sports and *Extreeeme* candy, extreme Christianity has become au currant, even trendy. Other fundamentalists need not apply, particularly the swarthy variety. Even moderate Sufi Moslems endure cavity searches at the local Post Office when sending Ramadan gifts to their family abroad. Jewish fundamentalists, politely tolerated when they ally themselves with their ideological partners in Christendom, are a non-issue in America since most emigrate to Israel, squatting in trailers in the fantasy West Bank neighborhood of the biblical patriarchs. Unfortunately, this is the contemporary neighborhood of millions of stateless Palestinians.

From the tent revivals and radio shows of the 20th century's populist prophets, through the humiliation of Goldwater's defeat in 1964 and the phoenix-like rise through the Reagan years, evangelicals reborn as "The Christian Right" have come of age and come into power in an unprecedented way. But despite its seeming supremacy and prevailing influence in Congress, the Presidency, and now the Supreme Court, the world view of the Religious Right is held by a minority of American citizens, even amongst eligible voters.

Good marketing, savvy manipulation of the media, and a strange bedfellow bond with Republican corporatism has successfully won elections, driven the national debate on culture, and convinced an entire generation of the struggling and dwindling middle class to vote against its economic interests to empower a narrow moral vision that spans *God, Guns and Gays* while our pensions atrophy, our health care rivals that of banana republics, and our corporate overlords continue to fill their coffers, denying their inferiors the luxury of buying, let alone eating, cake.

The 2004 presidential election provided a chilling

glimpse into the successful strategy of the ascendant Right. Claims to a popular mandate were rooted more in rhetoric than reality. Yet perceptions become reality if believed, and belief changes policy if it is said to represent the will of the people. The Right's actual agenda is obscured by its public face. It wields power but talks populist. It bangs the drums of war and trumpets the execution of the mentally ill while championing a "culture of life" for the unborn and terminally infirmed. It seeks to dominate the political process, employing the tactics of Tony Soprano to marginalize its rivals and squelch debate while playing embattled victim against coastal elites, cerebral academics, and the liberal-secular "cabal." Despite the Hellenistic, non-Christian origins of the concept, hubris increasingly defines the trials and tribulations of the Right as it balances the authority of Constantine with the humility of Christ.

The Christian Right set the tone from the start. As the 2004 voting booths closed and the ubiquitous exit polls sought to reveal the mysteries of the American electorate, the numbers seemed to vindicate the Republican strategy, the tireless efforts of the inspired faithful, and the very will of God in the hearts and minds of evangelicals. These results planted the seeds for the arrogance, obstinacy, and unilateral vision that tainted the unholy alliance between the Christian Right and the Bush Administration.

Two sets of figures told the tale and sealed the fantasy for many

~ *One quarter of the electorate were white, evangelical, born-again Christians who voted 4 to 1 for Bush*

~ *Asked about the issues that mattered most in their voting decision, 22% chose "moral values" as the definitive issue, and of that number, 80% voted for Bush.*

The Karl Rove/James Dobson matrix could not have conceived of better statistics to support their "non-reality-based" view of America. It proved two of their long-time contentions: That evangelicals were a decisive electoral force to be reckoned with, and that voters cared more about *morality* than war, the economy, or the education of their children (as if morality could be divorced from these issues).

Andrew Kohut of the Pew Research Center warned against drawing definitive conclusions from poll responses to the open-ended catchall phrase of "moral values," or the army of "values voters" who seemed to emerge from the shadows of cultural obscurity. The phrase "moral values" encompasses far more than the

Trite Trinity of the Right: abortion, stem-cell research, and gay marriage. Though 80% who chose "values" voted for Bush, 65% of the total polled supported some form of legal recognition for gay unions, and 52% approved of stem-cell research. And if a similar catchall of "economy" had been offered encompassing health care, taxes, jobs, and growth, 33% would have chosen this as their decisive issue.

Kohut pointed out that the number of voting white evangelicals remained unchanged from 2000 and did not reflect a growing revolution of faith. But it did reflect something important and often ignored by The Coastal Blue Empire, liberal think tanks, and the 527s that channel progressive passions. Beyond the usual suspects on the evangelical extremes, there are a growing number of people who regard faith of some kind as important and look to values, often rooted in Western religions, to inform their decisions and those of policy-makers.

Much has been written about the rise of fundamentalism in this country and beyond. The popular theologians Karen Armstrong and John Shelby Spong have examined these trends historically and theologically. The rise of Christian fundamentalism in this country is part of a larger historical trend, and while it reflects homegrown fears and strivings for answers to implacable questions, it is rooted in a global reaction to modernity, equality, and pluralism.

The theologian Martin Marty explains the world-wide surge in fundamentalism.

Around the world there's a massive, convulsive ingathering of peoples into their separateness, to protect their pride and power and place from the real or presumed threat of others. Almost always, this will be done on religious terms, because you want to use the highest level of ingathering.

Marty further describes the great, unifying threat and the extreme reaction to it using a familiar analogy.

...the forces of modernity reach everywhere... and it means that your social and personal identity is threatened...Fighting back is the big thing, and that's what everybody's doing: reacting, counter-acting. Fighting back. When you do that you've got to have heavy ammunition and you're not going to do it in a mild way. I've long been interested in religion and sports. There are no Unitarians or Reform Jews in the National Football League, but there are plenty of Pente-

costals. There are plenty of people who know
God's on their side and will bash the other guy's
face in God's name.

Moving from the sidelines to the factory, author
Robert Bellah adds a domestic ingredient to this simmering stew of reactionary discontent.

I think that the rise of the Religious Right cor-
relates with the first wave of the impact of glo-
balization on American society. Many Ameri-
can men that are pulled to the Religious Right
are people who have lost their well-paying labor
union jobs which had health care and retire-
ment, and now are working low-end jobs....the
Republicans, with their tremendous propaganda
machine, are able to turn this alienation, which
is rooted in structural changes in the American
economy, into a culture war.

The great irony, of course, is that while we fight a
global war on terrorism based in Islamic fundamentalism, and as we seek to export democracy and reason
around the world as remedy to this narrow medievalism,
we cultivate our own brand of religious extremism here

and provide it unprecedented access to the centers of power and influence.

While this irony seems painfully obvious to many, the Religious Right employs many tactics of distraction and dissembling to refocus attention on their agenda at the expense of the nation's welfare. One of the most effective is the Li'l Red Riding Hood/Big Bad Wolf politics of victimization. While pouting as the embattled Li'l Red Riding Hood amidst the dark forest of liberal/secular beasts seeking her destruction, the Right intimidates, coerces, and stifles challenge and dissent by bearing the fangs and growling the indignation of the Big Bad Wolf. The Wolf has eaten Red and is channeling her pleas for help from within its bowels.

This bizarre, schizoid identity was sent up by the primary news source for most under 40, Jon Stewart of *The Daily Show*. In response to an evangelical member of Congress who lamented the besieged state of Christian America, Stewart quipped

Yes, the loooooong war on Christianity. I pray that one day, we may live in an America where Christians can worship freely, in broad daylight. Openly wearing the symbols of their religion, perhaps around their necks. And maybe, dare

I dream it, maybe one day, there could be an openly Christian president, or perhaps, 43 of them...consecutively...Does anyone know... does the Christian persecution complex have an expiration date? Because, you've all been in charge pretty much since...what was that guy's name...Constantine? And he converted in ... what was it...312 A.D.? I'm just saying, enjoy your success.

Marty calls this bifurcated role of victim/victor the "politics of resentment," a residual sense of inferiority from years on the margins of popular culture. Even as this resentment has evolved into what Marty recasts as a "will to power," the scars of past derision and contempt at the hands of a left-leaning cultural elite continues to define how the Right views itself. What is most troubling and damaging for the future of our nation is the increased sense of polarization thwarting our ability to govern across the divide, rendering the political landscape a pock-marked battle field of winners lauding it over losers, and losers awaiting the day they can vanquish their haughty foes.

With the prophetic clarity of long experience, even Barry Goldwater, the patriarch of modern conservatism, warned of the encroaching influence of Christian fundamentalism. On the Senate floor in 1980, in words sanitized for the *Congressional Record* for their profane passion, Goldwater admonished

> *...on religious issues there can be little or no compromise. There is no position on which people are so immovable as their religious beliefs. There is no more powerful ally one can claim in a debate than Jesus Christ, or God, or Allah, or whatever one calls this supreme being. But like any powerful weapon, the use of God's name on one's behalf should be used sparingly. The religious factions that are growing throughout our land are not using their religious clout with wisdom. They are trying to force government leaders into following their position 100 percent. If you disagree with these religious groups on a particular moral issue, they complain, they threaten you with a loss of money or votes or both. I'm frankly sick and tired of the political preachers across this country telling me as a citizen that if I want to be a moral person, I must believe in 'A,' 'B,' 'C,' and 'D.' Just who do they think they are? And from where do they*

*presume to claim the right to dictate their moral
beliefs to me? And I am even more angry as a
legislator who must endure the threats of every
religious group who thinks it has some God-
granted right to control my vote on every roll
call in the Senate. I am warning them today: I
will fight them every step of the way if they try to
dictate their moral convictions to all Americans
in the name of 'conservatism.'*

Goldwater died in 1998 and thus did not witness the
fullest realization of his worst fears and the complicity of
his conservative movement in realizing the visions of the
Christian Right. We can only hope that the spirit of his
proud, independent political will lives on somewhere in
the movement he generated. Or we can hope that hubris,
the oft-learned lesson of the Greeks, can work its pagan
mojo on the meglomaniacally monotheistic.

Yet within this crusade for Christ lay the path toward another exile in the wilderness. But it is a costly exile, not only for those on the religious extremes, but also
for religion and faith more broadly in America. The Terri
Schiavo debacle in 2005 revealed both the arrogance of
the Christian Right in its desire to legislate morality for

families in crisis and the craven opportunism of partisan evangelicals who sought to use faith as political leverage against their enemies. The public responded with resounding disgust, and the 2006 congressional elections were, in part, an overdue comeuppance. As the idiosyncratic morality of a vocal minority confronts popular support for gay civil unions, stem-cell research, and levels of abortion rights, Reagan era social conservatives find fewer receptive ears for their brand of scapegoating cloaked in the pursuit of the sacred.

But when the Religious Right loses, something more important is lost. The 2006 congressional election punished those corrupted by the seductions of power to which any politician is vulnerable. While voters can reject the Religious Right's influence on government by casting out the politicians who have given it license to legislate, the credibility of formal religion and religious institutions suffers in the process. Many Americans increasingly separate a private spirituality and moral commitment to do good from the kind of "corporate" religious structure that seems hopelessly addicted to and led astray by power. Contempt and distrust for the compromised faithful extends beyond the obvious targets on the extremes, tainting perceptions of mainstream churches and synagogues that have long embodied the broader values of most people of faith. Liberal denominations are often lumped together with high profile mega-churches and "family-focused" movements as part of the Big Business of Faith.

This clumsy generalization of all organized religion into a contemptible Big Sancta, and the condemnation of the whole for the abuses of a few, threatens to obscure the good that emerges from religious ideals. As distrust for religious institutions increases, skepticism grows for the spiritual bequests of previous generations. Cynicism spawned by one kind of faith community becomes an indictment of the broader concepts of community and faith. This encourages a culture of the individual that views the world through the prism of a detached Seinfeldian irony, which, in turn, spirals into a greater sense of isolation. And when this contempt for faith and distrust of community subverts our inspiration to seek others as friend or helper, something greater is lost: our ability to relate to what lies beyond ourselves—a power and a purpose surpassing our reach and our gaze.

Yet a potent sense of the spirit, and a longing to realize the good that it inspires, endures through the cynicism, compelling us beyond a transient distrust for the current abuses of the tragically fallible. There must be a way to reclaim this passion and this purpose to insulate us from cyclical, inevitable disappointments in religious leaders and to reconnect us to the values, ideals, and aspirations that have enshrined faith as an indelible quality of the human condition.

The Myth of Secular Security

I don't know a died-in-the-wool, card-carrying, vow-taking, secret-handshake offering "secularist." I run in a diversity of circles and talk with people on all stops along the ideological spectrum. But I've never run across someone who would argue, let alone evangelize, the secular mirror image of the growing religious fundamentalism that is ascendant in our country.

A study estimated that there are 2 million self-identified "secularists" in our nation, representing less than 1% of the total population. This is hardly a groundswell for an emerging movement or organized conspiracy. Besides, secularists are by definition not joiners. If you buy the direct mail propaganda of the Christian Right or the best-selling bloviation of cable pundits, our nation is rife with secularist cells and cabals. And of course, a generous contribution to various conservative think tanks, family-friendly organizations and political action committees will assist in the grand resistance against the godless tastemakers of the rising blue tide cresting from both coasts over unsuspecting innocents residing in the wholesome floodplain of Middle America.

Christian Conservatives, and the broader conservative movement they currently dominate, are merely using a time-honored and highly effective method to unite their supporters and fill their coffers: the creation of a fearsome bogeyman. The myth of an entrenched and insidious secularist movement in this country has swayed elections, intimidated governmental agencies, and chilled the media into docilely embracing a narrow and superficial view of faith.

The focus of this crusade against the supposed rise of secularism is a critique of the constitutional basis for the separation of church and state. The real target of the Christian Right is not secularism but a pluralistic nation, one in which all faiths can flourish and none can dominate. "Secularist" is cast as epithet against anyone who suggests that school days should not begin with Christian prayers, tax dollars should not support religious institutions, and Mel Gibson's *The Passion of the Christ* was not a very good film (the line between taste and faith is often blurred on the Right).

The ACLU is held up as the ultimate agent of this secularist agenda. But in reality, it is joined by a host of mainstream faith organizations that cherish both religious ideals and the boundaries separating personal belief from public policy. This dogged insistence is not the morally perverse product of the permissive and hedonistic '60s. It is at the core of the political blueprint of this nation, forged by Jefferson, Madison, and their company of Deists who sensed the existence of a Grand Intelligence in the universe, yet sought to avoid the strife and bloodshed that ravaged Europe with its multiple, competing, state-sponsored embraces of God.

Today's demonized "separatists" are concerned not only about the influence of religion upon government, but also the corruption of religion by government. History reveals a troubling record of the church utilizing the state as enforcer for its unqualified vision for the world, often at the end of a sword or the fiery post of an auto-da-fé. Equally troubling is the tendency for temporal power in the hands of faith to pervert the conscience of religious leaders and skew religious principles for political gain. The inspiring values and lessons of faith become pale, empty husks of base enthusiasm when exposed to the seductive promises of politics and authority.

As a Jew, I am particularly pained by the damage wrought by the union of faith and power in the state of Israel. Far from the myopic mullahs of Islam's theocracies in sensibility if not in actual miles, Israel strives to be both a state of the Jews and a modern democracy. The structure of its parliament and the strategy of coalition-building give the country's smallest yet loudest voices a disproportionate influence over the majority of citizens. The people concede power to the ultra-orthodox, whose medieval take on the world is imposed on a primarily non-Orthodox population.

An Orthodox colleague lamented to me that Lord Acton's axiom well described Israel's rabbinic leadership: Absolute power corrupts absolutely. The financial scandals and petty turf wars of the official rabbinate reflect the dangers of too close a kinship between synagogue and state. Faith is more at risk for lasting damage and diminished credibility than a resilient and malleable government. There is a reason that most Israelis proudly declare their identity as Jews, but few outside of the traditional Orthodox enclaves would describe themselves as *da'ti,* or religious.

It is a lesson Americans should take to heart. Those who are most active in the cause of church state separation are not secularists who reject God and disdain faith. Rather, they are people of a progressive, pluralistic faith who cherish our experiment in democracy, defend it against religious coercion, and want to insulate belief from the corrosive effects of power. It is a noble enterprise worthy of our founders.

All stereotypes possess kernels of truth, rare examples to sustain them in the face of criticism, extending a faint aura of veracity to the claims of the exception as the rule. The same is true for the rise of secularism. The Religious Right will trot out the errant professor from some tiny liberal arts college, an articulate dread-locked refugee from a Phish concert, or the grass roots leader of a fringe non-profit as representative of the all-encompassing and iconic "Left." The media abets this misinformation by giving platform to these marginal views as the sole legitimate voice on "the other side" of the current debate over faith. Imagine the CNN split screen shot of a clean-cut Ralph Reed type defending the faith on one side, and someone looking like the love-child of Wavy Gravy and Phyllis Diller defending atheism on the other.

Most folks who question God's existence, if they are brave enough to reveal their doubts in this hyper-hosanna culture, are neither secularists nor atheists, but agnostics.

They are not arrogant or certain enough to completely deny God, declare the Bible to be fiction, or decry scriptural ethics as authoritarian control over the narcotized masses. Most skeptics, if they even think about it in a more than passing way, *just don't know.* They are open to the idea of a higher power, try to do the right thing, and want a peaceful and productive world for their children. But they are not comfortable making that leap of faith into unquestioning dogma and doctrine.

Agnostics would seem to present fertile possibilities for fundamentalists. Rather than demonize them as "secularists," the Right should try to convince them, through argument and example, that the way of faith is good for the soul and the world. *Isn't that the point of evangelizing?* Judging from the campaign emanating from conservative Christians and implemented by the Bush administration, it seems easier to raise the ramparts, rally the faithful, take no prisoners, and gather the spoils of the next few years, planting ideological seeds to take root in the coming generation.

Beyond the klieg lights and cross fires of the circus maximus of cable news, there are authentic secular treatises coming from the world of journalism and academia. Again, these are hardly grounds for a mass movement.

They are more like beautiful, artfully crafted scenes in a snow globe, placed on the shelf of interesting possibilities rarely to be taken down or examined in a way that will change anything all that much. Or they are like side-show freaks, literally scaring the *be-jezzus* out of us, standing as admonishing examples of the perils of a truly empty cosmos. Yet their existence in the great American conversation, still protected by a besieged Bill of Rights, evokes fascinating questions and compels the faithful to clarify their position beyond the comfy confines of the widely accepted.

One well-argued and thoughtfully expressed approach emerges from the philosopher Sam Harris' *The End of Faith*. The title itself is a throwing down of the gauntlet, adversarial, though probably necessarily so, in the current climate of religious fervor and competitive publishing. Harris presents a critique of religion that challenges our default positions, demanding that believers think through the relevance of their assumptions in the modern world. He confronts the role of religion beyond the American cultural wars to the twisted frames of Israeli buses, the bloodstained streets of Baghdad, and the smoldering ashes of the World Trade Center:

The concessions we have made to religious faith—to the idea that belief can be sanctified by something other than evidence—have rendered us unable to name, much less address, one of the most pervasive causes of conflict in our world.

We are painfully aware of the violent excesses of faith. But Harris argues that we are less aware of the damage we do to ourselves and to the world through our uncritical clinging to exclusionary myths as revealed truths. Even more troubling, he lays greatest blame not on narrow-minded, anachronistic, and even murderous fundamentalists, but rather upon the sagging shoulders of religious moderates who provide a secure buffer between the fanatical faithful and their rationalist critics.

Harris does not deny the human need for transcendence, but rather rejects unquestioned creeds and the horrors that have emerged from their more popular and pervasive forms.

The basis of our spirituality surely consists in this: the range of possible human experience far exceeds the ordinary limits of our subjectivity...
A truly rational approach to this dimension of our lives would allow us to explore the heights

of our subjectivity with an open mind, while shedding the provincialism and dogmatism of our religious traditions in favor of free and rigorous inquiry.

The iconoclastic writer Christopher Hitchens adds his potent voice to what was until recently little more than an abstract debate waged through the journals and websites of the intelligensia. Before he proclaimed the *Ungreatness of God,* Hitchens sharpened the incisiveness of his godless straight razor on the fundamentalist excesses of George W. Bush's post-9/11 America. In his critique of Alabama Supreme Court Justice Roy Moore's moral martyrdom for refusing to remove a two-ton Ten Commandment display from the courthouse atrium, Hitchens delves into the uncomfortable inconsistency of the Tablets for people who value both faith and logic. He challenges us to reconcile how the horrors of genocide, child abuse, and alcoholism could have missed the cut of God's top ten, while the ambiguous thought crime of covetousness echoes in our conscience as God's final pronouncement.

Like the negatives of pre-digital photography, Hitchens probes the possibilities of a polarized image of the current conflict

I wonder what would happen if secularists were now to insist that the verses of the Bible that actually recommend enslavement, mutilation, stoning, and mass murder of civilians be incised on the walls of, say, public libraries.

He adds a final burst of contrarian bravado, a proving sound bite to the Christian Right that is fodder more for cocktail parties than policy summits

…too many editorialists have described the recent flap as a silly confrontation with exhibitionist fundamentalism, when the true problem is our failure to recognize that religion is not just incongruent with morality but in essential ways incompatible with it.

The work of Richard Dawkins rounds out this marginal yet vocal trinity of celebrity atheists. A long-standing gadfly of scholastic scientism, Dawkins rides the wave of the current mini-backlash against fundamentalism that peeked through the polling of the 2006 congressional election. Dawkins takes a more strident tone than others, exuding a nastiness that goes beyond the shock of the publicity hound toward a genuine contempt for faith.

Irrational faith is feeding murderous intolerance throughout the world...[religion]...can lead to a warped and inflexible morality...faith acts like a virus that attacks the young and infects generation after generation...the scriptural roots of the Judeo-Christian moral edifice are cruel and brutish.

Dawkins' diatribes and Hitchens' recent screed, *God is Not Great: How Religion Poisons Everything,* are more insidious retorts to the American faithful. Ironically, in their venom and intolerance, they reflect the mirror image of the fundamentalism they decry. They have asserted a new Orthodoxy of Unbelief that views the majority of their global co-citizens as heretics worthy of an intellectual purification in the fires of strict rationalism. *New York Times* columnist Nicholas Kristoff is justified in his concern that the attention garnered by this militant neo-Atheism might revive a Christian Right humbled by the 2006 election. Dawkins, Harris, and Hitchens seem to play right into the stratagems of James Dobson, Mike Huckabee, and the remnant of Jerry Falwell's defunct majority, offering the high-profile adversary needed to invigorate their flagging fortunes. It is the perfect straw man for the chastened Right: iconoclasts who seem more powerful and influential than they truly are, combusting the smoke of an apparent danger free from the flames of a genuinely threatening movement.

Bertrand Russell, the scion of modern philosophical skepticism, offered a more thoughtful, grounded and eloquent critique of religion in his classic *Why I am Not a Christian*. His more inflammatory contentions, tame by today's standards, seem less reckless when emerging from the context of classical sources rather than the pot-shooting of the pundit circuit. Russell concludes,

Religion is based, I think, primarily and mainly upon fear. It is partly the terror of the unknown and partly... the wish to feel that you have a kind of elder brother who will stand by you in all your troubles and disputes... Science can help us to get over this craven fear in which mankind has lived for so many generations. Science can teach us, and I think our own hearts can teach us, no longer to look around for imaginary supports, no longer to invent allies in the sky, but rather to look to our own efforts here below to make this world a better place to live in... Conquer the world by intelligence and not merely by being slavishly subdued by the terror that comes from it... We ought to stand up and look the world frankly in the face. We ought to make the best we can of the world, and if it is not so good as we wish, after all it will still be better than what these others have made of it in all these age.

The notion of secularism itself is far more nuanced than the extreme pronouncements of the atheistic media darlings or the knights of faith opposing them from the right. Scholar Alan Wolfe brought secularism back to earth in a recent article in *The Atlantic*. Wolfe rejects the established poles of secularism v.s. faith, positing that "secularism is not the opposite of belief; nonbelief is." He traced secularism through John Locke's utopian vision, rooted as much in Enlightenment ideals as in Protestantism, finding that "In contemporary societies influenced by Lockean ideals...religion's priority of belief and secularism's commitment to individual rights are not in opposition; rather, they complement each other."

In reality, very few people would identify themselves as devout secularists to pollsters let alone friends and family. I would venture a guess that there are more self-identified Wiccans than secularists amongst the

American electorate. Even those who celebrate the implications of a truly god-free world do so more out of a need to boost subscriptions, sell books, or engage our great American pastime of shit-disturbing than as a mission to put to sleep our next Great Awakening.

So what about the rest of us, those who are neither absolute nor apathetic in our faith? Many feel deeply about matters of the spirit, but for one reason or another do not formally affiliate with a community or ideology. Yet spiritual matters and moral values play a significant role in their lives. Where does a person who finds morality in a broader faith go to escape the chilly emptiness of godless rationalism, while condemning the craven descent of public expressions of faith in the service of power and wealth?

Gimme "Spirituality"

It can happen amongst the tinkling glasses of a cocktail party, in the quiet confidence of my study, or if I'm truly unlucky, on a transatlantic flight when the only film is *Dirty Dancing 2* and the void aches to be filled by anything else, even a captive conversation. After the Chicken Kiev is cleared and all the magazines are read, the discussion invariably turns to my chosen vocation.

The floodgates of conscience burst open. People seem compelled to confess to me, even though Judaism lacks this formal mechanism for expiation: "Rabbi, I haven't been in a synagogue since my Bar Mitzvah, which wasn't the best experience. I really don't like crowds, the fashion show of the High Holidays, or the fact that Temple life seems to be all about the money."

These are legitimate, but easily processed complaints. The most frustrating thing, of course, is that these folks have determined that synagogue life, and by extension anything that Judaism has to offer, remains unchanged since they were in 7th grade. Stranger still, their relationship to God, to community, and to the principles of faith hasn't evolved beyond the perceptions of a 7th grader. Think about where you were in 7th grade! Imagine if you operated now with the worldview you possessed in 7th grade. I'd still be wearing three-piece disco suits, avoiding hard candy to protect my braces, and sweating profusely anytime I came close to a girl and a scratchy version of "Stairway to Heaven" on a turntable. Hardly a firm foundation for a full and varied adult life!

Eventually my confessors deliver the punch line: "You know, I'm not religious. I don't like organized religion. But I'm very spiritual, and that's what's important." The unspoken postscript: "I'm still a good person." I'm never sure exactly what they mean, and I suspect they share my uncertainty about their ambivalence. But I can intuit through their inability to speak with precision. They want the inspiration that comes from faith, the anchored security of tradition, and the uplift of fulfilling worship without the demands, obligations, and responsibilities of formal membership in a community. At the risk of sounding too harsh, too much like Dana Carvey's angry old man on *Saturday Night Live* ("In my day…."), they want what we've come to expect in modern culture: Instant Fulfillment. Or to borrow John Lennon's take on it, they want "Instant Karma."

There is a huge gap between those who formally "affiliate" with churches and synagogues and those who would tell a pollster that they have faith in God. A recent Pew Forum poll offered a profoundly diffuse, post-denominational picture of the faith of many Americans: Up to 44% switched religious affiliations in their lifetimes, and the fourth largest "religious group" (16%) is the unaffiliated. And of the unaffiliated, 70% said they believed in God! Again, despite the fairytale presumption of conservatives that this augurs a growing secularist fifth column, the unaffiliated profess a faith that defies the classic categories of atheism or agnosticism. They identify with a more personal, less institutional movement characterized by pollsters as "nothing in particular."

In my region of the Pacific Northwest, this disconnect is most pronounced. Of the 40,000 Jews who live in the area, only 20% join congregations. Yet I bet most would say that faith plays some role in their lives. They are caught in a spiritual bind. They've given up on the religion of their parents, but they sense that there is something essential in us that seeks something beyond this world. They describe their faith as "spirituality," and religious sociologists have described this cohort as "seekers." They are often baby-boomers who have *been there* and *done that*. They have come full circle through Landmark, Buddhism, hedonism, and recovery to arrive at the point they associate with their parents' stable and satisfied middle lives, with spouses, children and mortgage in tow. Yet they lack the bonds of community and tradition that sustained the previous generation through tough times and magnified the joys that give life ultimate meaning.

Often these "spiritual seekers" will reach out for something, anything but the "organized religion" they dismissed as children. They find pale substitutes in the self-help aisles of Barnes and Noble, the flights of fancy of long-dead science fiction writers, or the low-commitment variations of Judaism, Christianity, or Eastern religions that amount to little more than the next generation of savvier, more clever cults.

But the pursuit of spiritual experience is more than mere trend and fashion. It is a real, increasingly documented human need. The emerging field of neurobiology has begun the process of proving, on a physiological level, that we are hard-wired for faith. This is the next step in the evolution of the social-scientific study of religion, embraced most notably by Sigmund Freud's studies of faith as neurosis, Carl Jung's analysis of unconscious communal symbols and rituals, and Joseph Campbell's description of heroic myth as inspiration for a half dozen Star Wars films.

New technologies allow unprecedented scans and analyses of the brain. Andrew Newberg and Eugene D'Aquili offer a spiritual map of our psyche in their book, *Why God Won't Go Away*. Through a fairly comprehensive explanation of the structures of the brain and the origins of perception, these scientists hypothesize "...that spiritual experience, at its very root, is intimately interwoven with human biology. That biology, in some way, compels the spiritual urge."

They assert that our brains evolved an ability to sense and seek transcendence beyond the material world, and that in our ability to perceive and process what lies beyond our noses, the world of the spirit is no less "real" than the physical world.

...God cannot exist as a concept or as reality anyplace else but in your mind. In this sense, both spiritual experiences and those of a more ordinary material nature are made real to the mind in the very same way—through the processing powers of the brain and the cognitive functions of the mind....all that is meaningful in human spirituality happens in the mind. In other words, the mind is mystical by default.

Perhaps one explanation for the 70% of Americans (see below) who have ultimate certainty of God's existence lies in the folds of gray between our ears. Again, Newberg and D'Aquili provoke our convolutions.

Evidence suggests that...religions persist because the wiring of the human brain continues to provide believers with a range of unitary experiences that are often interpreted as assurances that God exists...the strong survival advantages of religious belief make it very likely that evolution would enhance the neurological wiring that makes transcendence possible. This inherited ability to experience spiritual union is the real source of religion's staying power. It anchors religious belief in something deeper and more potent that intellect and reason; it makes God a reality that can't be undone by ideas, and that never grows obsolete.

This would partly explain the dissonance of those who pursue spiritual experience on the one hand, but are skeptical about established religious order on the other. We are driven to seek spiritual experiences, and when we are unable to find them around us in convenient or relevant forms, the entrepreneurial spirit steps in to fill the vacuum. Or we are left in a limbo of unrequited apathy that, if left unabated, descends into a cynicism infecting other aspects of our lives, sickening our sense of self and self in the world.

Pop culture only exacerbates this faith-bind through its normal course of over-simplification, hyperbole, and shallow romanticism. I'm at the tail end of the baby boom, and love the creative genius and social conscience of a Dylan or a Lennon. They have ascended into the pantheon of contemporary icons, often described as "prophets" to a generation that, ironically, derides biblical prophecy as fairy tale or form of authoritarian social control. The message, model, and manner of these pop prophets send mixed and confusing signals to a congregation of listeners searching for higher meaning in literary lyrics.

Bob Dylan has test-driven more religious vehicles than Jeff Gordon has Nascars. He dons them like the wide variety of outfits he's worn for three decades, conflating a dilettantish exploration with spiritual depth in the hearts of eager acolytes. An interview with John Lennon revealed the ideological evolution that accompanied his lyrical progress. He moved from "Love is the Word" to "All You Need is Love" to "Give Peace a Chance" to "Imagine," with its utopian dream of "no religion, too." Lennon implied that this represented a kind of personal and philosophical growth, from teen lust to hippie idealism, from political activism to the Olympian heights of the unity of all and the distinction of none. That's where he arrived when he was killed, frozen forever as sacrificial lamb to the vision of a world without borders. But it is also a world without boundaries, without identities, a world that does not transcend human nature but naively defies it. While this works for the trippy tendentiousness of the late-night dorm room and provides fodder for the hipper of academic colloquia, it is weak broth for spiritual sustenance.

The media doesn't help when it chooses to give open mics and dominant voice to the extremes of the spectrum. A casual sampling of talk shows and news programs reveals that the axiom still holds: "If it bleeds, it leads," or in this case "The craziest creed leads." The ravenous, ever-moving maw of the 24/7 news cycle constantly seeks the most over-the-top, stereotypical spokespeople and stories to portray any issue. One is more likely to see protesters beating each other with signs over a picket line than to view a dispassionate discourse on the history of abortion and its ethical implications. You have to reach far back on the newsstand, past the computer rags and male-oriented soft porn to find a journal with a nuanced, two-sided presentation on a key issue. When faith comes into the crosshairs of the corporate media machine, when it is the issue of the moment because of a recent poll, or an election, or a manufactured moral crisis, the damage to views of faith endures long after the shark has moved onto the chum of the next movie star marriage debacle.

In more subtle moments, the media still portrays faith in simplistic and inaccurate terms. The *New York Times*' coverage of a referendum on gay marriage in Spain demonstrates this quest for easy, imprecise conclusions. Popular support for gay marriage was characterized in the newspaper's bolder, larger font as "the rise of secularism" encroaching upon southern Europe from the chilly, godless north. Further down in the body of 8 pt. font there is a different account.

In the article, a Spanish sociologist saw in the church's lament fears of losing a grip on political power, an authority over the masses it possessed since Ferdinand and Isabella booted the Moors and Jews out, rendering Spain a second-rate sovereignty ever since. Studies found that 80 % of Spaniards identified themselves as Catholic, though 20% never go to church and 50% go only for weddings and funerals. As an arm-chair sociologist, I would attribute this more to the Spanish church's 50 year history of giving cover to fascism than state sanction of the guys next door seeking to tie the knot.

The gay marriage vote is part of a larger trend in Spain, where previous controls over divorce and in vitro fertilization have been lifted, and the school system's mandatory classes in Christianity have been augmented by exploration of other faiths, including Islam, which happened to be the country's dominant religion for eight centuries. While church pundits see this as a decline, most of us in the democratic west would embrace this as a judicious balance of freedom and faith.

Other analysts of this moment in Spanish social history see the strength and endurance of family as weakening the traditional allegiance to the church. In Spain, many under 35 still live with their parents, and weekly family gatherings are common. Ironically, the strengthening of family is one of the key contributions of religion touted by its advocates. But what if a culture empowers family without the church? And what if the church actually becomes an obstacle to family wholeness? An uncomfortable conclusion is drawn in the *Times* piece.

> *As acceptance of homosexuality has grown, many Spaniards have considered it more important to assist gay relatives than to listen to church doctrine, said Fernando Vallespin Ona, president of the Center for Sociological Investigation. "Spaniards love of their children is deeper than their love for their religion," he said.*

An Ipsos/AP poll on global views of faith offered fascinating insight into the spiritual views of different nations. One of the results was particularly interesting. In the U.S., we spend like the French but believe like Mexicans. We consume like the first world but seek God like the third world. Regarding the importance of religion in our lives, only the U.S. and Mexico chalked up percentages in the mid 80s. The range of responses to belief in God, from complete disbelief through doubt and uncertainty, showed 70% of U.S. respondents and 80% of Mexicans testifying, "I know God really exists and I have no doubts about it."

Not surprisingly, social and religious conservatives touted the poll as proof that America is a God-fearing nation, far more devout than comparable Western nations. The assumption extended to an implied support of the Christian Right's agenda. The less reported figure was in response to the influence of religious leaders on government. In the US, 61% opposed this breach of boundaries, and in Mexico a whopping 75% found it wrong for clerics to dabble in civics. While conservatives can celebrate the declared faith of their fellow citizens, they should not assume it to be a defined or even recognizable faith.

While the poll makes no distinction between belief

in God and affiliation with religious institutions, the rejection of religion's role in the formation of public policy is a marked criticism of the current crusade of the Christian Right in our country. Belief in God is strong in America, but support of the established order as a pathway to God is far less certain. Many sense an awareness of God and seek to translate that into some meaningful presence in their lives. But the form of that awareness and the function of that presence are not clear or concrete.

We have forever left behind the time when established religion defined absolute truth and exerted absolute power. Modernity has brought with it new freedoms for the human mind and spirit but also new seductions, many of them harmful and tragic. In the marketplace of ideals and beliefs, traditional religion is one of many that must compete for attention and relevance. The outcome of that competition will determine nothing less than the course of our civilization.

There is cause beyond coercion that classic religious wisdom and ritual outlasted other attempts at inspiration and meaning. Religion speaks to something enduring and essential to the human condition. People long for a faith that speaks to emotion and intellect, offering opportunities for growth through service that are so compelling that, if taken seriously and embraced genuinely, can be life-transforming. But the wellsprings of faith must slake the thirst for relevance and transcendence, guiding us to live well in this world while inspiring us with a power beyond this world. If established religion continues to operate as if it's the 15th century, it will become obsolete within the 21st century. But if the only alternative is to pander to the vacuity of the culture, to meet only the transient needs of the self with disposable values divorced from a sense of responsibility to others, then our faith will possess all the endurance and stability of a sandcastle.

This will be a tragedy beyond the inevitable passing of institutions and ebbing cycles of history. The refusal of religious institutions to adapt to contemporary spiritual needs is a betrayal of a millennia-long chain of tradition, of those who preserved the wisdom of faith at peril to their lives yet understood that a living faith must evolve to respond to the ever-changing, ever-growing human spirit.

To borrow, with far better intentions, the paranoid words of Richard Nixon, spiritual seekers and others like them represent a "silent majority" of people who long for a fulfilling faith life and supportive faith community but cannot find a place for these feelings or an object for this search. They believe that they are alone, surrounded by others who seem to have their acts together, who seem happier and more satisfied. In reality, these frustrated and disappointed walk amongst a large and growing congregation of the lost and longing. It is perhaps the largest community of faith in our nation. Its numbers swell by the day, and its ideals are quickly eroding into a cynicism that will do far more harm to our society and its future than the current bogeymen that pique our fears, pry open our wallets, or con our votes.

As *New York Times* columnist David Brooks observes, the knock-down-drag-out between pop-skeptics and spiritual shock troops over the existence of God is but the first event on the cosmic fight card. The main event in this epic battle is far more rigorous in its demands and far more indelible in its impact.

The real challenge is going to come from people who feel the existence of the sacred, but who think that particular religions are just cultural artifacts built on top of universal human traits.

We are at a crossroads between apathy and idealism, between continued search and deflated dreams, between an optimism rooted in an undeniable spiritual need and the tragic possibilities of widespread neglect of the soul. I hope the following will bring some degree of hope and contentment to many who have not found a home for the spirit and those who have outgrown their current spiritual home.

Spirit at the Center

EVEN IF WE HAVE A HARD TIME DEFINING IT, MOST OF US CAN DESCRIBE A MOMENT OF TRANSCENDENCE IN OUR LIVES. For many, it is the classic "aha" or "whoa" moment of a sunset at the Grand Canyon, the birth of a child, or a sense of paradoxical oneness amidst a large crowd of like-minded folks, often at a Grateful Dead show or NCAA tournament game. I had a series of these feelings through the summers of my adolescence while attending a Jewish camp.

As the son of a rabbi (a description, not a pejorative in this case), I was quite conflicted about my belief in God and view of religion. With the limited maturity of a teenager, I both immersed myself in the life of the synagogue while denying its importance in my life. For the most part, I sought to embarrass my father with my shallow skepticism and smart-ass response to well intentioned yet annoying inquiries about my future. I insisted that not only would I not be following in my father's footsteps, I made a point of demonstrating beyond all doubt that I was in behavior and attitude the least likely candidate to enter the rabbinate. There was more than one Sunday school teacher who fled the classroom weeping.

That was during the year. In the summer, something remarkable happened. In the forested depths of the Santa Cruz Mountains, I found God and found a calling. Nothing dramatic or miraculous. There were no horses at this camp. Falling from one would have been a nightmare of litigation and insurance claims, and the closest Damascus was in Idaho. But gradually, as I matured and the years passed, these annual immersions in faith amidst natural beauty changed me. I was not alone. The Jewish camping movement of all denominations has produced more rabbis than the preceding three generations of synagogue services and rabbinic sermons.

Though we joked about the cult-like intensity of the experience, this was far from a rigorous, controlled climate. It was effective because it perfectly blended a young person's longing to discover self in connection to others with age-appropriate and engaging exposure to Jewish values and practices. There were plenty of sports, swimming, and pursuit of young lust. But there were also entertaining and substantive programs on Jewish history and culture, hands-on work with talented artists, and the gentle guidance of older counselors who grew up in the system and whose passion inspired them to return the favor to the next generation.

But what most moved me was the worship. If the educational programs were miles ahead of the limited offerings of the Sunday school classroom, the worship experience was light years beyond the staid *shul* show of the '70s synagogue. As we welcomed the Sabbath on Friday evenings, the entire camp would don white to gather as a community on the center lawn beneath the large boughs of coastal redwoods. The dappled sunlight and shadow marked well the boundaries between the coming holiness of Shabbat and the receding sameness of the past week. We joined arm in arm in large, seemingly endless concentric circles of friendship and communion.

Most of these kids came from families of H20 Jews: *Holidays, two only.* Yet they looked forward to these worshipful moments. Brief but meaningful prayer services were infused with creative readings and relevant applications of ancient values. The Sabbath dinner was a distinct and memorable fare of barbecue chicken, green beans and carrot cake. And after dinner there was a song session, at times as raucous as a roomful of drunken cha-sids, at moments possessing a sweetness and sensitivity that belied the numbers and ages of the chorus. Forging the wisdom of little known sacred writings to the melodic, familiar idioms of '60s folk music, these songs were at the heart of what made camp distinct. They inspired the inexperienced and the apathetic to unexpected levels of spiritual feeling and communal connection. These formative summers still reverberate for the generation that came of age during this era, shaping expectations for worship and education amongst those who long for their children to be moved in the same way.

As I look back upon a lengthening tenure as rabbi, I still find those camp summers to be some of the most significant spiritual experiences in my life. Yes, I was young and impressionable. But there was something more to it than wide-eyed idealism. Dr. Mary Dell, an adolescent psychiatrist and Episcopal priest, credits the emerging spirituality of teens to their developing understanding of abstract concepts and expanding sense of empathy, "In religious terms, this gives them the ability to discern between institutional religion and an internal relationship with God." I certainly felt this as a teen worshipping amongst the pungent redwoods, arm in arm amidst a sea of white-clad, sun-tanned bodies, singing moody melodies to timeless words that touched me in ways that were overwhelming, ways I only now fully appreciate. This kind of prayer linked me to others, and to God through others, in ways that continue to resonate, ways I constantly long to recreate for others and myself.

This sense of spiritual satisfaction is not merely a quality of youth. It is not innocence or naivete that, once jaded by adult disappointments, frustrations, and narrowing of perceived possibilities, cannot be rekindled. We need not accept the stark choice between the "childlike" dreams of the world that can be and "adult" acceptance of the "real" world as it is. Eastern religions seek to recapture a childlike sense of wonder, not as regression to an immature stage, but as an acknowledgement that the young possess a powerful vision of possibility that the journey to adulthood can diminish.

Our ability to feel this connection to others, to the world, to something beyond the world, sometimes simultaneously, does not calcify at 12 like the ability to learn language. It resides within each of us as individuals and as links in a chain of community that extends in space across the globe and in time through the generations. For many it lies dormant or atrophies, and it is this unrealized and unmet need that evokes frustration and cynicism in so many of us. Judgment is skewed to pursue fulfillment in the nonsensical, the addictive, and the destructive. And after the smoke of search clears and the mirrors of narcissism are cleansed, we remain unsatisfied, feeling even emptier than before. Yet there is an itch left unscratched, a hunger left unsated. It is a need that if ignored will produce a sickness of soul as palpable and damaging as any to the body.

The marketplace is filled with remedies and panaceas for this emerging illness. Our culture of confession, often televised and twisted as pain for profit, vents the bile but rarely offers healing and wholeness, promising that public declarations are the key to private redemption. Books and websites, and the movements and programs that spawn them, temporarily provide salve to the pain of misuse and disuse of this significant part of the self. More often than not these are only distractions, setting out 7 steps on the path to 70 more, pointing the way to a lengthy journey guided by common sense cast as the profound, often bringing the seasoned seeker full circle to the place where he began, not any wiser but certainly poorer of cash and less hopeful for having taken the trip.

In our contemporary culture of speed, static, and searching, even the most well-established and time-tested systems must vie with an unprecedented smorgasbord of activities and ideologies to rise above the cacophony, to register awareness. To allay the suspicions evoked by emerging forms of spiritualism, clever marketers mask their sometimes silly, sometimes dangerous departures in the comfy cloak of tradition. The Jewish mystical system of Kabbalah, long derided and ignored by a rational, assimilationist, and modernizing Jewish community, has had a resurgence amongst scholars and serious students. But it has also been commodified by entrepreneurial charlatans, who sell salvation in blessed bottled water and self-assurance in the fraying threads of a red wrist band, yours for only $29.95 on Target's website.

There is much theo-tainment taken too seriously by the otherwise bright and savvy. A despair of the soul leads many to check their brains and healthy skepticism at the door. The new numerology reveals divine insight through acrostic play with sacred scripture, predicting 9/11, the Iraq War, and, when the fifth letter in each verse of Genesis is read diagonally, forming a dire warning about the fall of Fannie Mae. Ancient sages are channeled through failed insurance brokers to counsel ailing marriages and encourage the purchase of a 5-DVD box set on fine-tuning the shakra through green tea enemas. And the biblical mandate to help the poor is perverted into an up-by-the-boot-straps affirmation of avaricious capitalism or a prosperity gospel that dulls yuppie guilt by answering the trite question of "What Would Jesus Do" with the tragic answer: BUY!

Many are surprised that true direction and genuine growth can be found in the least likely of places: the hoary traditions of our youth. But like Oldsmobiles and corporate pensions, this doesn't have to be your father's faith. The faith communities that endured through the ages were those that integrated timeless values with contemporary need. Those that didn't evolve with the times died. Their histories are fodder for Ph.D. theses, arcane symposia, and *Jeopardy* categories. The belief systems that survived spoke to the concerns that defined people's lives in the moment, yet inspired them with the credibility and authority of the ages.

Despite the ubiquity of pop-up window promises of heaven for 90 days same-as-cash, there are exciting, legitimate opportunities to realize the rabbinic axiom of "pouring old wine into new bottles." Many creatively plumb the depths of established traditions, discovering ancient practices and principles purged through the ages by hierarchical politics and selective heresies. These approaches neither pander to current fashion nor dilute principles that constrain the appetites and impulses of our current celebration of the extreme and the instantaneous. This renaissance of faith reflects a growing awareness, well understood and abundantly appreciated for millennia, that God's revelation is ongoing, a renewed sharing of the eternal and the absolute made relevant to each generation. The relationship borne of this revelation determines how God lives through us in the world, and most importantly, why.

In his bestselling history and challenge to Islam, *No god but God*, the hip, accessible Muslim celebro-scholar Resa Aslan cites the not-as-hip theologian Harvey Cox's distinction between *secularism* and *secularization*. *Secularism* is a narrow, almost fanatical commitment to the creation of a godless society. *Secularization* is an evolutionary force that encourages an ongoing ceding of power from the historical seat of the church to the more pluralistic and inclusive authority of the state.

Similarly, there is a difference between indoctrination and inspiration, between uncompromising fanaticism and affirming faith. The values and ideals of the spirit can evoke conscience and provoke action without threatening individual freedom or becoming co-opted by machine politics. Finding this balance requires a deliberation of mind, an examination of heart, and a commitment to engaging all in a debate and dialogue that, though painful and emotional, can bring about a more just, more peaceful, more whole world. As the rabbis teach, "All arguments for the sake of heaven will be fulfilled."

With humility and hope, I offer a suggested course for a challenging moment in our history. It is a course rooted in the traditions of monotheism but aware of the need to liberate its wisdom from the shackles of human frailty and fear. It assumes the presence, power, and concern of a central entity that can be called "God," who was revealed many times in many ways, forging covenants as myriad as the people who sought and found answer. It is a template that can be grafted upon both formal belief and an undefined sense of the ineffable. It is a call to come home to a place as ancient as it is novel, as intimate as it is all encompassing, as deeply ingrained as it is challenging to comprehend.

Spirit at the Center

The concept of **Spirit at the Center** can be a bit ambiguous, not to be cryptic and mysterious, but to reflect the uncertainty that we all feel in the presence of the indescribable in our midst and in ourselves. Each of us encounters the concept differently, bringing different needs and stories, gleaning different lessons and value from our struggle to comprehend, own, and live out its mandate. Yet it is the great task, the great challenge of theology to forge community consensus from individual experience.

There are two basic assumptions that arise from Spirit at the Center. The first envisions a life lived with matters of the spirit at the *center of our being.*

Center of Our Being

There are, in turn, two components to **spirit at the center of our being.** The first is an awareness of a power, a process or a being greater than us—***The Creator of Spirit.*** Mysticism is for the masses. One need not sweat through hot yoga or bathe in chilly waters to induce a mystical state of awareness of the divine. Some of my youngest students ask me why God seemed to speak all the time to biblical figures and never speaks to anyone today. My answer: *God is speaking all the time. We've simply not made room to hear.*

Moses, Jesus, and Buddha lived in simpler, quieter times. Sure, you died from an ingrown toenail, but there wasn't the pressure to fill every moment with stimuli. For a carpenter, farmer, or shepherd, there's not much to do in the evening other than tell stories around the fire and listen to one's thoughts. Today's diminishing attention span amidst an increasingly distracting culture produces too much static, too much noise. God could take a bullhorn to our conscience and it would fade into the background of carpools and commutes, ipods and the internet.

Imagine the difference between the night sky viewed from the heart of the city and the constellations seen in the country. The ambient city lights blur out the majesty of what is there all along, if only we would move to a place with a clearer view. In the ancient world, every night sky impressed with its panoply of brilliance and possibility. But astronomers were not the only visionaries inspired by nature's light show.

When the heroes of our sacred myths sought a direct experience with God, is it any wonder they left the city and headed for the desert, the mountaintop, or the base of a rural tree? Through moral genius and mystical insight, they brought their experiences back to an often stubborn and obtuse world, creating an accessible pathway to the infinite and a simple, disciplined method of realizing the power of that encounter in the world. The greatness of the founders of faith emerged from what they created out of that experience. Yet we all can share in it. Awareness of the sacred is a sixth sense, and like touch, taste, and sight, it can be dulled by disuse.

If our ancestors needed to leave the village to find clarity to sense the sacred, how far must we go? Escaping the city or taking other kinds of leave from our hectic lives provides space to appreciate and revel in other parts of the self we give short shrift in our daily grind. The concept of the Sabbath emerged to provide a weekly refuge of the spirit for people who could ill afford or had little opportunity to get away physically. As imagined by the modern sage, Rabbi Abraham Joshua Heschel, it is a refuge in time, not in space. It provides respite from the toils and troubles of the week to embrace the best, most essential parts of the self. The Sabbath enables us to tend to the most neglected, most integral of our relationships, to heighten awareness of the eternal, ever-present Divine abiding within us, coursing through us, surging around us, and reaching beyond us. To better appreciate the *Creator of Spirit*, we must craft our own versions of this Sabbath refuge in our lives.

But "God" is only a name, a tool of thought and expression we use to convey a concept, to point to an ideal. Many are put off by an unwillingness or inability to accept the traditional idea of God that has inspired and driven, perplexed, and persuaded so many. Yet while rejecting the concept of a defined "God," the uncertain often acknowledge a force in the universe beyond chance—a craftsmanship that implies a Creator, an ordered structure that assumes an Architect, and a great purpose that reveals a Grand Intelligence. Though they may depersonalize this idea, rendering it a power or force rather than a defined, singular entity, it remains distinct and apart from the created.

This distinction between what "is" and its "cause" compels a relationship. Some see this as a onetime exchange, Newton's cosmic clockmaker who gave reality a vigorous twist and lets us ride out the Great Unwinding. Others see constant, daily interaction with the infinite, not in Spielbergian encounters atop a mountain or the DeMillean halving of large bodies of water, but in the subtle, nuanced daily gifts that surround us, often ignored in the triage of what we deem "important" at the moment. A languid apathy, a broad uncertainty, or even a strident rejection of the divine concedes a relationship to that which is neglected, confusing, or threatening.

While this may seem an argument from the negative, it is a time-honored theological tact to deduce that which *is* from that which *isn't*. In seeking to know God, classic theologians relied on the *doctrine of negative attributes.* We can more reliably list the qualities that *are not God* than those which *are God.* Like throwing darts at a bull's eye we'll never hit, but hopefully home in upon with each successive attempt, this doctrine is an honest concession to our limitations in truly knowing the *Creator of Spirit.* Yet it is a critical step toward an authentic encounter, the first level of Spirit at the Center of Being.

Quid pro quo, the fundamental idea of "something for something," is as key an ingredient in the neuro-chemical stew simmering in our skulls as is receptivity to the mystical. From the prehistoric bartering of Neanderthals on the savanna to the torrential maelstrom of the Chicago Options Exchange, life is a series of deals, commitments, and cost/benefit analyses. It is not surprising that this essential part of the human condition would make its way into an understanding of faith from its tribal origins to the highest reaches of formal theology.

This forms the second component of **Spirit at the Center of Being: Promises and Expectations.** In highfalutin' theological language, this idea is called *covenant.* The infinite, transcendent "Other" shares our understanding of exchange and obligation. Whether this is objectively "true" of God or merely our limited take on what we imagine of God, the result is the same. Contact and communion, discussion and dialogue are only the first step. Something more must grow from simple exposure to what is bigger and beyond. Throughout our lives, we are changed by our experiences, transformed by our relationships. How much more so are we changed by our experience of God! Whether we ignore the bond and its impact or embrace it, we become different in the presence of the infinite. And like the storied founders of faith, we, too, can bring something of this moment back to our world to better our lives and the concentric circles encompassing the lives of others.

Contemporary belief and doctrine have moved well past the ancient, unreasonable demands of capricious gods who could only be sated by human suffering and who sought entertainment at human expense. The sacrifice of children to Baal on flaming pyres and the prospect of Zeus transforming into a swan seeking sex with unwitting maidens have mercifully morphed from core theology to intriguing anthropology. These views of the God/human dynamic reflected the world of our ancestors, who led lives the philosopher Thomas Hobbes imagined to be "nasty, brutish and short." The gods of the ancients were well suited to that life.

God evolved as civilization and culture evolved. Again, whether this was an actual change in the essential nature of God or the development of a deeper, more complex understanding of God to accompany our more sophisticated understanding of the world is beside the point. Perceptions change when God is viewed from different points in history. Revelation is ongoing, adapting to contemporary need and ability to comprehend. The infinite is infinitely mutable. We seek in God what we lack in ourselves.

Those of us who aspire to be good or merely decent seek to balance personal comfort with poignant conscience sensitive to the plight of others. We seek love intimate enough to enrich our lives but comprehensive enough to change the lives of others. We seek a moral purpose that will guide our path while inspiring a broken world to find direction and healing. And God, whether mirroring or informing our intentions, reflects well our current priorities and perspectives.

The text, traditions and rituals that preserve an ongoing understanding of God through the generations are a mixed bag. They possess timeless values, the product of moral and spiritual genius relevant to any generation. But they also contain triumphalism, xenophobia, and exclusivity, qualities that characterized the ancient world that imprinted the authors and conveyors of tradition. For all the clarity of consciousness available in the uncluttered world of the past, there was much superstition, fear, and rage to cloud the mind and muddle the message. The challenge for the modern person of faith is to implement reason and to plumb conscience to filter the message in two ways.

First, one must separate the precious kernel of divine insight from the husk of the society and times that shaped the fallible people who crafted the message. And second, one must distinguish the words and wisdom of God from the human ambitions and agenda of the self. This is no easy task. It requires knowledge of history and an honesty of self that few of us possess intuitively. It demands a seriousness and discipline in short supply in our culture of solutions found in popping pills at a pace to match the time it takes to load a large webpage with broadband. But it is an accessible insight for those who are able but yet to be willing.

The core message of faith, uncovered through this archaeology of the spirit, is rooted in both communal consciousness and personal insight. Once embraced emotionally and intellectually, we find that God does not demand that we jump through irrational and nonsensical hoops for esoteric reasons understood only by an elite priesthood. Engaging awareness evokes deeper understanding, which fosters enduring belief. But we are accustomed to the give and take of the human marketplace and expect God's demands to reflect the benefit provided: a wondrous world, a stable reality, and the opportunity to grow, live, and thrive beyond mere existence. It is a tall order. If God lacks nothing by definition, what can we offer God in exchange?

The answer: *God wants what benefits us.* Maybe this is a convenient creation of God in our own image. But wouldn't we expect ultimate altruism from a being that out of infinite kindness and with infinite power created a reality It did not need and could have "lived" without? We can wax cynically, arguing that caring for the world and its inhabitants is the coerced response of the fearful, placating a tyrant's fragile ego. Or we can conclude that God is concerned only about the welfare of Creation as work product. But that is to envision a fairly petty deity, a pitfall Job encountered at a time of extreme personal challenge when even his justified complaint met with God's frustration and impatience. Is it so unreasonable to expect us to care for a world so meticulous in its planning, so exquisite in its execution, so enduring in its echoes of eternity?

We are offered a strange and wondrous covenant, reflecting the ideal relationship, modeling what human relationships could be. Though none of us is perfect and powerful like God, the lesson of giving not for obvious return, but for the larger wellbeing of the whole, is worth learning and living. The stakes of this covenant are simple and universal, but the terms and structure are what often divides us. Some believe that we earn credit in this world, garnering frequent flier points for a first-class ticket in the next. Some believe that we are cosmic debtors, seeking to pay back through our lives the blessings bestowed on us in the simple, powerful act of creation.

And there are many, the followers of both a formal path of faith and more free-form seekers, who believe that we do good in this world to make this world the best that it can be. The silent majority of spiritual-seekers-without-affiliation often relies on this secular, philosophical argument. It contends that the pursuit of an ethical life and a moral society is a boon in and of itself. Unsure of the existence of God, these seekers are fairly certain of what constitutes good in the world. While this may work well on one level to compel behavior and encourage order, it lacks a critical component. It depends entirely on contemporary standards of good and is rooted too narrowly in a personal sense of what is right. These standards can vary across generations and around the globe. And this sense is often driven by convenience, responding more to the needs of the moment than the welfare of the world.

Contemporary mores and personal criteria can inspire and contribute to the greater good, but they are insufficient. What is lacking is *accountability*. Not a tyrannical submission to authority for its own sake, as millennia of clerics demanded in appropriating temporal power to protect corrupt religious systems. Not a concession to discipline as needed character trait, the hobbyhorse of social conservatives who envision God as a belt-wielding, stern father figure. There is something qualitatively different, deeper, and richer when we act in the world in response to expectation than when we do not. Maybe it's rooted in our infantile need to please our parents. Or maybe that universal need of all children exists to prepare us for a greater challenge: to meet the expectations of a greater power toward the achieving of a greater goal, a greater good.

Accountability arises from consensus, an agreement

that some things are the same for everyone at all times. But consensus is not conformity. There is room in the infinite mind of God and the complexity of the human spirit to harbor both the creative diversity of civilization and the unity of progressive purpose. With myriad cultures each containing myriad individuals, all with hearts and minds differently directed toward what lies beyond, what lies within, and what's to be done, we seek some common vision, some absolute truth.

It is a truth that is absolute less in its power to persuade than in its promise to redeem. It is a truth embodied by the One Who brings together all, Who is shared by all, Who encompasses all. It is a truth that anchors our sense of responsibility by focusing it on tasks that compel humility. It is a truth that conveys expectations that inspire us to rise above the baseness of what *is* to imagine the greatness of what we *can be*. The accepting of these responsibilities, tasks, and expectations becomes a fulfillment of covenant with the Infinite and balm to an ever-troubled world.

An awareness of this transcendent, some would say "sacred" responsibility, is a constant whether we acknowledge God or not. Even the most stridently secular recognize the value of joint, concerted pursuit of the good. But when we set this responsibility within the context of covenant, winnowing down the terms incumbent upon us to those that are clearly good and possess a truth apparent to communal standards and individual conscience, a truth absolute in its resonance and overwhelming in its possibility, and when we see on the opposite side of the existential divide a caring and conscious Other who seeks to build relationship, any endeavor before us gains a power and purpose of cosmic proportions. Our contributions, large and small, of great note and anonymous, become part of a good beyond mere benefit and exchange. Our work in the world becomes integral to the wholeness of the world, and we grow to be more than good people striving for a good world. We join in partnership with the One from whom we came. This is what it is to have *Spirit at the Center of our Being.*

Center of Ideology

A famous quote from Abraham Lincoln aptly describes the second assumption of **Spirit at the Center: Spirit at the Center of Ideology.** Lincoln knew well the uses and abuses of God to justify the most divergent of moral positions. In his time, God's will and grace were invoked to support both the institution of slavery and the abolitionist movement. And if sacred scripture was the only true source to discern God's will, how could it endorse opposing moral poles? Amidst this cultural schism made real and bloody through years of civil war, Lincoln famously admonished the belligerent parties. As always, his purposeful references to God, nuanced and thoughtful in their subtly, far more effectively forged God's sanction to human intent than the crass chest thumping of today's refugees from tent revivals. Lincoln intoned, "My concern is not whether God is on our side; my great concern is to be on God's side."

The current cultural divide also emerges from conflicting visions of society rooted in the role that religious principles should play in the public square. Though hardly as devastating as the Civil War, the extremism engendered by our current moment threatens to compromise the delicate balance crafted by our Founders to insulate the national vision from particular creed and to protect rarefied faith from the seductions of statecraft. It is an extremism borne of fear and insecurity, as it has always been. The post-9/11 world looms with threats both real and imagined, requiring serious defensive measures. But appeals to base fear and its malicious handmaiden, concession to prejudice, have served the interests of power and paralyzed the progress in civil and human rights begun in the last half of the previous century.

We have always reached out to God as protecting, nurturing parent, and to the comforting guidance of faith at times of greatest need and darkest night. The absence of atheists in foxholes exaggerates an essential, documented human longing for answer and meaning when the ways of the world confuse, the fickle finger of fate mocks, or a sneaking suspicion creeps over us that there's no one at the wheel. Out of arrogance and lust for control, we try to regain a sense of power over our lives. Embracing a paradox that only the human ability to rationalize could endure, we mask in humility our confidence in absolutes: our absolute understanding of God's will and our absolute capacity to realize that will most authentically in the world.

In its most severe form, this paradox takes the form of fundamentalism. Fears of the modern, its alienation and displacing of the individual, its celebration of the material, and its imperial, wireless encroaching upon even the most far-flung corners of the globe drive new generations of radicals to embrace nostalgia for a past that never was, compelling a vision for a world that can never be. It is a vision of a world coarsely cloven into good and evil, a world some will die to bring about through smoke and blood.

The symbiotic seduction that weds power to faith finds a less extreme but still troubling form in America. Selective and sectarian takes on religious values amplify a nationalism that compels both an adventurous foreign policy with imperial designs and a domestic agenda ironically echoing the pre-modern world view the global crusade for democracy seeks to vanquish. The drafting of God to embolden particular vision and to empower partisan agenda arrogantly perverts the universal message of faith and profoundly cheapens divine revelation into political hackery.

Like Lincoln, a serious and honest search for God, embrace of faith, and realization of its ideals for the world compels us to move toward God's side, not drag God to our side. God is diminished, faith distrusted, and its ideals belittled when we view them as a means to the end of our purposes and priorities. The truly faithful seek God openly, read texts critically, and bring divine wisdom to life with an uncompromising generosity that transcends an uncompromising rigor.

If we truly embrace God as the object of our ultimate love and devout appreciation, if we aspire to implement divinely inspired values to enrich an incomplete world, if we seek to become unqualified vessels of this apparent truth free of our petty schemes and self-interested strategies, then we must strive to make real this ideal through authenticity of message and humility of purpose.

As mentioned previously, a part of our struggle with scripture and tradition is reconciling the conflict between revealed values and personal convictions. These are sometimes in concert and require little more than contemporary tweaking and modification to be made relevant to current need. But at times we arrive at a metaphysical and moral fork in the road. We can mold our lives to values that challenge us to rise above our base impulses and appetites, looking to a criterion beyond convenience as our compass. Or we can plunge into the lukewarm waters of rationalization and delusion to justify departures from the strictures of the spirit as necessary and timely, allowing us to call ourselves people of a faith *we* inscribe and seal with God's imprimatur.

If we are serious about the ethical system emerging from faith, we must maintain the integrity of the message of faith, recorded in scripture and tempered by tradition through the creative interpretation of human genius. We are heirs to this process, receiving revelation in our hearts and minds, digesting and owning the message through critical analysis and spiritual transformation, and implementing the message in our lives and in the life of the world as a sacred synthesis of divine power and human ingenuity.

But we must take care not to permit our personal needs and desires or the ideological demands of the group to subjugate the message of faith, and by extension the Originator of the message, to mere justification of our will. This requires a profound awareness of self, a scrupulous honesty borne of this awareness, and a strength of character to distinguish the voice of God from the seductive demands of trend and tribe. It is a task that has overwhelmed even the most altruistic and austere of biblical exemplars and religious leaders. But even when heroes, saints, and martyrs fall and rise again in the service of God and to the benefit of their fellows, the lodestone that keeps them on course is humility.

Once we have done our best to purify our limited but valid understanding of the message of faith, cured in the fires of reason and conscience, stripped of the detritus of personal and partisan agendas, it is the rare quality of humility that enables us to live lives of faith as model and to inspire others to do the same as lesson, with some degree of credibility and authority. It is an authority that derives not from power, but from the promise of extending the goodness we experience to others. It is a credibility that grows not from persuasion, but from the potent truth exuding from a life lived well, a life that seeks well-being for others.

One might expect humility to be a prerequisite to discerning the pure message of faith and not the converse. But we humans are not born to be humble. It did not serve our evolutionary purposes when the law of the jungle held sway and only the strong survived. Humility is one of those rarefied values, cultivated and lauded by human beings. It was part of an effort to "civilize" human beings through culture and creed as they made the transition from primitive hunting party to diverse community.

Humility is bred, not born, and it is found only in the higher levels of consciousness and awareness. It requires an appreciation beyond the fundamental needs of self, family, or nation. It encompasses a vision of the self as a part of something singular and greater, something of which we are a precious part, but something which transcends the sum of its parts. Humility emerges both from the substance of scripture/tradition and from our approach to these carriers of spiritual message. This is a theological Catch-22, but we can embrace and transcend the paradox. The message of humility becomes clearer to us when we approach the message humbly. We become more humble as we imbibe the message.

The message of and process toward humility is a profound example of what makes scripture more than a merely human device and invention. Though written and edited by human beings and imprinted with human foibles, scripture imparts superhuman demands and ideals that are challenging yet attainable. Its delicate balance of divine prohibition and command, denial of self and affirmation of life, demonstrates how scripture is both of and beyond humankind. Whether inscribed by fiery finger at Sinai or expressed with literary precision and moral potency by those inspired to commit their spiritual experiences to writing for the ages, the call to live out human ideals like humility is at the crossroads linking divine will and human ability, what we are and what God wants us to be.

This is a powerful message, possessing truth that is useful beyond utility, truth that is right beyond choice, truth that is empowering beyond ego, truth that overwhelms us, not to intimidate, but to hone our perspective as creatures in service to God through service to the world. Our aspirations toward ideals are an experience with the divine essence in a form that is accessible, comprehensible, and the ultimate way to meet God in daily life.

Spirit at the Center of the Ideology enables us to focus on the challenges of the world towards achieving not what is merely in our best interest, but what is in God's best interest for the world. This centrality of spirit helps us to see through the priorities of the here and now to the timeless challenges that link past to future. These challenges evoke a wisdom implanted deeply within our consciousness, inspiring a response that can be freed from its moorings in the ancient world to be made real and relevant today, reflecting more than a mere 12 steps to self-actualization, partisan plank-crafting for an election year or as basis for the excesses of nationalism.

The next section will trace how the concepts of *Spirit at the Center of Being and Ideology* can inform our understanding of current challenges and inspire righteous action toward a repair and healing of the world—a building upon strengths and successes, and an honest confrontation with our weakness and failures. Though not exhaustive, there are three key global concerns that will demonstrate how a *Spirit at the Center* approach can provide a new context for the many who seek to imbue life with faith: economic justice, the environment, and peace.

Just Do It

Nike commercials are among the most effective and evocative. They are short, punchy, and memorable. You don't even see the shoe clearly until the end. Nike is selling an attitude, a passion, perhaps even a life philosophy. Quick cuts link glimpses of athletic excess: Lone runners surging down foggy paths, panting to the methodical steps of their jogging gait; a free rock climber's fingers straining against a ledge in a cloud of grip-aiding chalk dust; a soccer player muscling his way down field amidst a cacophony of opponents' grunts and screams that sound more like the beach-landing scene of *Saving Private Ryan* than a spectator sport. And then…. the screen goes black. The famous swoosh materializes followed by three words: *Just Do It*.

Just Do It. Summing up both Nike's goal of associating their product with physical discipline and achievement, and pointing to a larger challenge resonating within most of us. We love to plan and prepare, envision and deliberate. Often the means becomes the end, as process paralyzes us, and we rationalize our inaction as necessary to a goal we'll never achieve. For some it's learned procrastination or inherent inability to pull the trigger on anything in their lives. For others, it is fear of the unknown, the difficult, the challenge that can define a depth of character we'd rather not know we lack.

But when it comes to important things, personal goals upon which our healthy growth is based, or social and global struggles for which our support is critical to a just outcome, apathy and inaction become more than amusing foibles or annoying habits. They are the difference between the world as it is and the world as it can and should be.

Negligence of our own spiritual education and experience leads to apathetic concession to a world we'd rather not live in, but one we are resigned to tolerate. Judaism is one of the most practical faith traditions. We can find God on a misty mountaintop or in the quiet meditative moments of a worship service. But Jewish values are only meaningful if we've studied and owned the sacred myths recorded by previous generations. And the individual transformation that emerges from heights of piety and depths of study is only fulfilled if we devote the transformed self to changing the selves around us. It's not enough to feel faith and think deeply. We must act definitively.

This obligation to act is simply yet powerfully conveyed by the Hebrew word for Jewish law: *halacha*. Halacha is rooted in the Hebrew word for "walking." Jewish law is the *way to walk*, to *do* in the world, to move ourselves and our surroundings forward. The Torah scroll itself reflects this pragmatism. This sacred revelation is not shrouded in esoteric mysteries that only a cabal of priests can decipher for the unwashed and uninitiated. Torah was designed by God to be accessible and applicable.

Large tracts are devoted to the minutiae of civil laws covering property rights, personal liability, and the dynamic tension between authority and citizen. But in Judaism, civil law is inextricably enmeshed with ritual law. There is no clear separation between ethical and religious obligations.

The Torah is the practical blueprint for the society to be created by Jews when they reach the Promised Land. But this is not just any society: it is to be a holy society, in covenant with God, committed to the wellbeing of the divinity embodied by each of us. Laws governing behavior within a society are actually the terms of the deal forged between this people and their God. These laws transform the practical and the necessary into the sacred.

This concept, though uniquely Jewish in many ways, can inform and inspire all who seek to bind social responsibility to spirituality, to ground morality in something more than the pursuit of the merely good. Morality, at its best, at its most powerful, is rooted in the pursuit of the holy.

What follows are a few key ways in which *Spirit at the Center* of both our *being* and our *ideology* can change our context as profoundly as our core—our surroundings as meaningfully as our soul. But we must put aside cynicism and apathy, conceding less to what can't be done and committing more to what can be done. A voice more awesome, words more indelible than the tag line of a Nike ad appear on the scope of our inner vision, hopefully to even greater effect than the mere selling of shoes. Just Do It.

Mirror Mirror

It's the kind of moment a parent hopes and prays for. But until it happens, we are uncertain and a bit insecure about what will result. For many American kids today, overfed, overindulged, and distant from the daily life-and-death struggles that afflict millions, the face-to-face confrontation with poverty and suffering gauges whether secure privilege can empathize with privation. Does the warm, rarefied insulation of *having* confound the developing moral compass from seeking, let alone finding, the *have nots*?

Our family was walking around Union Square in San Francisco during Christmas Week, the embodiment of social and existential paradox. Union Square is the high-end shopping center of one of the most financially inaccessible cities in America. Over the years, "The City" has devolved into a tapestry of socio-economic extremes: a residential haven for the obscenely wealthy interwoven with conspicuous, abject poverty. Union Square is within blocks of The Tenderloin, the city's Bowery West. An evening of fine dining and multiple glasses of wine can turn ugly quickly with a wrong turn toward a forgotten parking lot.

But even the best efforts to keep these adjacent streets and worlds apart are futile. Domestic divas cloaked in Vera Wang and enraptured by store windows join Armani-clad Masters of the Universe entranced by Blackberries in a feat worthy of a perverse Olympic Games: stepping over the homeless while maintaining both stride and concentration on anything but the unpleasantness beneath their Blahnik and Ferragamo-caressed feet. It takes remarkable physical skill and exquisite moral myopia to traverse a sidewalk of suffering while focusing exclusively on the next boutique, an ongoing Pacific Rim business deal, or a chance for a five dollar double machiatto.

While it's painful to see how the city has changed, I still wax nostalgic for its progressive past as capital of the counter-culture. Elements of this past still reverberate in certain coffee shops, music venues, and artsy urban enclaves, but much has been subsumed by the nouveau-within-a-nano-second-rich. But San Francisco will always be, to some extent, my home, and I enjoy sharing that sense of return with my children.

A walk down memory lane provides a life-lesson in the harsh realities of a cloven society. I'm torn between parental instincts to protect my children from these worldly inevitabilities, a futile impulse as old as the longings of Siddhartha's father, and the desire to heighten awareness and stoke empathy for the lot of so many in the world, the key to the young prince's transformation from pampered elite to exemplary Buddha. Not that I hope to raise young Buddhas myself. I'm happy if an overworked teacher can cram a few sessions on the Indian Godhead into the World Civilizations curriculum at my daughter's middle school. But gleaning a bit of moral insight from street experience is critical for any sheltered suburban Siddhartha to become even reasonably enlightened.

As we were walking along the square, the unusual and the pathetic lined the way like a sideshow of the downtrodden. The needy know with precision where the money is and where to seek the most likely source for conscience-stricken income: vacationing tourists. Some merely sit with plaintive signs desperately etched on stained cardboard, recounting a life story in miniature or summing it all up with an existential plea: "Hungry." Others try to ply their case and pry open hearts with genuine feats of musical skill or uncanny ability to stand statue-like for hours covered in robotic gray paint. Still others lack talent but show heart through banging a paint can or singing a tune badly, seeking to offer something more than an empty hand in a world driven by an ethos of quid pro quo.

I tend to give to organizations that effectively provide for those in need, striving to bring the homeless and the hungry back into the dignified, purposeful world of work. On occasion I will give to people on the street. But I feel conflicted. Am I perpetuating their dependence and supporting their ability to continue to live at this subsistence level? Empathy usually trumps principle, and when I'm with the kids, I jump at the chance to model an obligation to others.

This is a lesson I am proud to impart to my children. But it is usually unnecessary. Within about half a block, I feel a tug on my arm. "Daddy, look at that man. Why is he here? I want to give him something." I'd like to feel that I have consciously passed on these precious life lessons and nurtured these poignant qualities in my children. But truth be told, it is in them from the beginning, as if still-undiscovered markers on strands of DNA are predisposed to empathy and indignation. I provide them a few dollars to give, or we buy too few sandwiches to pass out to too many recipients. But in significant ways, my kids are changed, just a little. And maybe the world has changed, just a little.

Perhaps the great ideals of scripture and tradition are merely affirmations of what we already possess. Divine revelation doesn't teach us as much as it reminds us of values long forgotten to consciousness but forever inscribed on conscience. In this remembering, we are emboldened to embrace and express the best part of ourselves. It is a lock longing for a key to open its hidden power, a seed awaiting the cool waters of inspired faith to saturate the fertile soil of another's need.

The New Atheists often criticize biblical principles as unnecessary. Wouldn't we know that murder is wrong, that adultery and robbery are harmful to society even without the Ten Commandments? Indeed, these are renowned and universal proscriptions. But history is filled with much rationalization of conscience and relativism of social norm. We have an uncanny ability to justify almost anything in pursuit of what we want and to conform any law to a perceived good. We need not look far in the past to find the most infamous and egregious examples of human life sacrificed at the altars of charismatic leadership and national passion.

The good and the holy are within us. Scripture and tradition inspire and empower us, through the experiences and efforts of those who came before us, to limit and channel the biological urge toward the self and amplify the higher, more-than-human aspiration toward others and "Another."

The hardwired empathy my children feel and the

urge to do something about it are given voice through God's vision made real in sacred words conveyed by human hand and heart. Two ideals rooted in these texts provide us with the courage and compulsion to seek need beyond ourselves. Each conveys a facet of *Spirit at the Center* of *being* and *ideology*. They are *b'tzelem elohim*, the recognition that we are created in God's image, and *ve'ahavta l're'echa kamocha*, the demand that we love our neighbors as ourselves.

The famous verse from the first chapters of Genesis proclaims that we are created *b'tzelem elohim*, in the image of God. Not surprisingly, human arrogance read this inspiring bit of wisdom conversely and shallowly. God must look like us, we thought, envisioning physical images that spanned Michelangelo's steroid-infused Kenny Rogers-like Creator, to an unassuming George Burns as borscht-belt therapeutic deity, through a more diversity-conscious depiction of Morgan Freeman robed in the white linen suit of a maitre'd at a Miami spa. The narrowness of mind to assume that God looks like us is surpassed only by the lack of imagination inherent in conceiving that the essence of God is physical at all.

It surprises some (too many) to learn that the ancients and medievals were far more comfortable and conversant with a metaphoric interpretation of sacred text than today's *bibliolaters*—those who worship text as if it were God. A literal reading of the Bible in light of growing human awareness, science, and God-gifted common sense was/is the delusion of the unlettered, the unsophisticated, and the loony. Great pre-modern theologians like Maimonides, Aquinas, and Averroes understood the concept of God's image as far more significant than what can be represented by imperfect, degrading flesh. They saw our best qualities, our loftiest potential, and the most intangible but essential parts of the self as being cast in the image of God. Call it soul or consciousness or animating spark. The ability to discern and act morally, the compulsion to act beyond self-interest for the welfare of others, and the longing to make the world something better than it is are traits worthy of reflecting God's image. It is the impactful yet intangible nature of these qualities that renders them, and us, most like God. The sense that our values and aspirations reflect God in this world is integral to a Spirit at the Center of Being approach.

The punch line at the end of the Holiness Code within the 19th chapter of the biblical Book of Leviticus is a revelation that is universal, simple, and yet elusive. Chapter 19 begins with God's message to the people,

"You shall be holy for I YHWH (God) am holy." The Hebrew for holy is *kadosh*. *Holy* is one of those fuzzy words that mean different things to different people. In Judaism, it connotes that which is *separate* or *set aside* for special purpose. The Sabbath is set aside from the rest of the week to temporarily cease our obsession with the mundane and to confront the neglected parts of our lives. The Hebrew word for marriage is *kiddushin*, connoting a separation of another from all others for a unique intimacy, connectedness, and love.

So God wants us to be holy. Seems simple enough. But with even a bit of further thought, we really don't know what we are being asked to do. The text anticipates this confusion and continues with a list of real world acts that define this bewildering command: from leaving the corners of our fields for the poor and disenfranchised to not taking advantage of those whom we might exploit; from rendering justice without concern for the pressures of power or sympathy to releasing heart and mind from the death grip of grudges.

And the punch line, the closed bracket at the end of the list which sums up the true nature of holiness: "*ve'ahavta l're'echa kamocha*—love your neighbor as yourself." The rabbis who interpreted this verse hundreds of years after it was crafted saw a foundational concept. A rabbinic legend has a clever jerk visiting two famous rabbis, Hillel and Shammai. Hillel was the more lenient authority, and not surprisingly the more popular and beloved. Shammai was a bit of a stickler who did not suffer fools easily.

The trying traveler approaches Shammai, and standing on one foot, asks to be taught the entire Torah. I love picturing this flamingo-like refugee from a Monty Python movie aggravating this crotchety, beet purple old man on the verge of an aneurysm. Predictably, Shammai admonishes this perceived fool with a stick, probably more for wasting the great man's time than for posing a ridiculous query.

This inquiring mind next sidles up to Hillel with the same question on the same foot. Hillel, a teacher known as much for his knowledge of tradition as for his insight into human nature, replies: "Do not do unto others as you would not have them do onto you. All the rest is commentary. Go and study." The legend concludes with the silly skeptic becoming a pious student.

Jesus proclaims something similar, but both stories are reiterations of the Leviticus text that at its core is a key religious value enshrined by most faith traditions and communities: the sanctification of compassion. To love your neighbor as yourself is more than merely "walking a mile in another's shoes." It requires deep reflection, an awareness of self that compels an honest accounting and clarity of purpose. Before we can learn to regard and treat another like ourselves, we must better know ourselves. We must learn to love ourselves.

And after transforming the self, we cannot be contented with personal success. Sharing the benefits and blessings of self-discovery is integral to its ultimate fulfillment. It is only in the turning to another that we find the true capabilities of the self. It is only in the turning to another that we nourish the spark of the divine within us.

And then there's love. We tend to have a limited view of love. We love our family and friends. We fall in love, romantically love, and confuse lust for love. But if loving our neighbor as ourselves is essential to being holy like God, then our love for another is akin to our love for God. It is mysterious, rooted in ideals that transcend this world, challenging us to feel more inclusively and extend ourselves to unprecedented lengths.

We love God as a mighty sovereign who uses power judiciously and selflessly. We love God as a parent who nurtures our growth, endures our mistakes, and supports us throughout our lives. We love God as a force of nature, encompassing the physical universe and existence. But God is a natural power with a moral intention. God is an intelligence and consciousness Who cares for us as profoundly as It governs the universe, a power that is as intentionally good as it definitively drives the progress of time and space.

But for many of us, from the marginal believer to the agnostic, this love need not be a personal bond with a distinct entity. There is wonder and reverence for the remarkable order and structure underlying *the way things are.* There is an intuitive sense that there is stability, honor, and purpose in striving to bring goodness, healing, and well-being into the world beyond instinctive self interest. Call it God, call it the Force, or call it Doing The Right Thing. It is the awareness of what should be done, the commitment to doing it, and the discipline to make it happen.

It is tough to love another limited, faulty, and physical person as we love the Infinite and the Good. But when we love our neighbor as ourselves, we love a piece of that Power and that Purpose within another. This love heightens our awareness of that same Presence within ourselves. Thus, we bind the self, the other, and God in that sacred, dramatic moment when we transcend the here and now, moving beyond our singular needs to embrace the needs of others as part of an interdependent reality. This recognition of others as part of a beloved whole imbues earthly acts of goodness with cosmic ramifications.

This seems to be an easy, humane, and eminently decent approach. Yet this simple extension of empathy and compassion has gotten twisted and obscured by the growing culture war in America. What would otherwise be a more substantive debate in religious or philosophical circles in support of policy-making has been bound, gagged and run through the sausage grinder of the media-political complex to feed the faux self-righteousness of mandarins of morality and pandering candidates. For them, religion is narrowly defined as the puritanical assessment and condemnation of anything the self-appointed doyennes of faith decide is beyond their parochial experience or close-minded views.

The fundamental role of compassion in all religions, perhaps one of the few ideals all faith communities purport to share, has been obscured by this rush to judgment, or worse, it has been selectively offered to the few groups deemed acceptable by virtue of their abject privation. If Jesus had been as discriminating toward the objects of his comfort-giving, he might be remembered today only by leper colonies.

The need to embrace a more inclusive theology of compassion towards economic justice is well expressed by the Spirit at the Center approach. And more importantly, an embrace of compassion as the center of our spirituality restrains and re-channels narrow minds and wasted energies spent giving in to our tribal fears of the unknown, our rejection of those we deem "other." Faith at its best helps us to rise above our base human impulses rooted in our animal origins. Faith inspires us to be more than human.

Seeing this through Spirit at the Center of our Being reminds us that what we share most with others is both beyond the physical and is that which is most essentially who we are. When I'm asked about the Jewish view of life after death, I respond with a blend of personal views, medieval philosophy, and mainstream theology. While seemingly divergent, these three streams of belief actually integrate well.

I start with a shocking assumption. Our bodies are about $212.34 worth of chemical compounds (adjusting for inflation). But if you think about it, what makes us most who we are, call it spirit, soul, animating force—the source of imagination, memory, personality, and self-reflection—is not physical. Sure, scientists can monitor the sloshing around of neuro-chemicals in the brain. But they cannot quantify or qualify the sum of consciousness that is profoundly more than its parts.

This part of ourselves—in many ways the most identifiably *us* part of ourselves—is not physical. Yet it is more *real* than the physical reality that we assume is *real*—the reality filtered through our system of perceptions, interpretations, and analysis. And it does not go the way of all physical things when the body dies. It may transform or evolve, but it endures.

Now, here is where this afterlife narrative breaks down. But does it matter? There is no certain destination for that soul or consciousness. But who cares? If a key purpose of religion is to assuage fear of death, isn't it comforting to know that what makes us most who we are will continue in some way? Will our disembodied soul, free from the constraints and struggles of the physical, actually obsess on the earthly concerns of process and goal?

Yet spiritual insecurity has compelled us to fill the gaps. Rather than accept a more authentic belief filled with questions, we fashion bizarre fantasies and frightening imagery to provide answers that try the credulity of even the most faithful. We'd rather imagine a Heaven like La Costa and a Hell like a Shiloh Inn on the Pennsylvania turnpike than settle for the unknowable. Perhaps true salvation lies in contentment with who we are and who we will always be, rather than in worrying about where we're going and whether we'll get a non-smoking room.

And that essential understanding of who we are and who we will always be binds us to others in the most intimate and universal way. Whether we call it God, or divine spark, soul, animus, or neuro-chemically induced electrical energy, we share it with much of the living world, and most closely with all humanity. I always liked the explanation I heard for the Japanese custom of bowing: that one is honoring the divinity in another. Even if it isn't accurate, it's true.

The biblical authors intuited this when they taught from the very, very beginning that we are created in God's image. This was more than a literary wrinkle in yet another creation myth common to the ancient Near East. It is a perspective fundamental to our worldview and our place within it. It is our shared patrimony, the ultimate secret handshake to the most inclusive club, an imprint as discernable and more elemental than our DNA. It is what binds DNA and gives it purpose.

And these authors bound self-awareness to an awareness of the needs of others through the command to extend love beyond the self. There truly is no *us* and *them*. We are inextricably linked to God and others in our longing for comfort, dignity, and happiness. *Holiness* is dependent upon *wholeness*. The recognition that all are one, that the ultimate well being of each of us requires the well being of everyone, compels us to turn self-awareness into just action.

With Spirit at the Center of Being thus defined, the next step to Spirit at the Center of Ideology flows naturally. If the self is suffused with, even composed of, an essence that both transcends and unites us, than we should strive to recognize, honor, and support that essence in others. We can chose not to do so out of negligence, apathy, or even cruelty. But reaching out to the spark in others that we know within ourselves is more than a pursuit of good. It is a kind of self-preservation. The self, physically and spiritually, cannot survive alone, and must seek out and sustain others to survive. Psychologists and anthropologists assert the social and emotional benefit accrued. Neuroscientists can even plot brain activity in pleasure areas associated with giving to others. Whatever the reason, it's remarkable that loving our neighbors as ourselves is both selfless and self-serving, that pure altruism can satisfy individual need. We can have our cake and share it too. It's too convenient not to have been planned, whether enacted directly by supernatural fiat or simply observed as law of nature.

Even a cursory, History Channel-based survey of civilization reveals the limitations of the law of the jungle, of "looking out for #1." Animals are far too consumed with feeding, breeding, and fending off threats to turf to empathize or consider others. Humanity really took off as a going concern when we started to cooperate, organize, share, and divide labor. The societies that sought shortcuts by reverting to the modes of the wild kingdom stagnated or died. Those who struggled against this default to the lowest human denominator, channeling animal impulses to reach heights attained only through critical thinking and moral awareness, bequeathed to us the best in art, culture, scholarship, and folklore. Again, when our ancestors mastered the self to serve others, they not only sustained themselves, they evolved.

This view, rooted in some of the oldest ideas to emerge from faith communities, formed the basis of the kind of pluralistic, modern, and civil society we both take for granted and are often forced to defend. The European

Enlightenment crafted and championed the "unalienable rights" we assume today as quintessentially American, a fact that neo-conservative critics of "Old Europe" conveniently forget. But it did not take piety and devoutness to recall and re-establish this eternal truth. The deistic notions of the founding fathers, which consciously and deliberately excluded specific religious traditions, acknowledged the supernatural origins of the natural rights endowed in all of us. While the clarity of Greek philosophy gave this democratic system structure, it left it abstract and impersonal. The Patriotic Pops sought an accountability that transcended the merely utilitarian. One need not call it *God* to recognize that it is something both not of this world and essential to this world.

These rights become something greater than inspired thinking and impassioned rhetoric when we act on them. And nothing is more fundamental to human existence than physical wellbeing and the sense of self that emerges from living well. Economic rights are the basis upon which all other rights depend. Spirit at the Center of Ideology compels us to secure the comfort and dignity of others. And in this shrinking global village in which interdependence is a fact rather than a progressive talking point, domestic concerns for economic opportunity are inextricably bound to the global call for economic justice.

While *charity* is a noble concept, it is insufficient in that it depends on the irregularity of good will. Charity is rooted in the Greek word *karitas*, which connotes a loving regard for others. It smacks too much of noblesse oblige, of the matron deigning to bestow crumbs from the family table upon the kitchen help. The Jewish notion of *tzedakah* is rooted in the Hebrew word meaning *justice*. Love is preferable, but beside the point. There is an obligation to give, not out of desire but out of necessity—cosmic necessity. It is a requirement of the covenant with God, a relationship founded on an agreement that defines us. It is a seeking of justice for all rooted in the basics of what it is to feel human: to have a roof over our heads, food in our bellies, and an ability to live a life of purpose rather than to merely endure existence.

Call it a spiritual tax, for this conveys the necessity of shared burden in seeking common good. Even science confirms this moral assumption. A recent University of Oregon study demonstrates that paying taxes tweaks some of the same pleasure centers of the brain as giving to the needy. And while this may irk those who pervert the Bible's message to support regressive tax codes, the yanking of one's own bootstraps, and the unrestrained rapaciousness of Enron-era capitalism, it is essential to the very Jewish message that Jesus embodied. But one needs neither Jesus nor Judaism to embody this Spirit at the Center of being and center of ideology. One needs only a willingness to make it real in our lives and make it matter in the lives of others.

The Ultimate Rent for the Cosmic Landlord

After a long morning of worship on Rosh Hashanah, the Jewish New Year, the tradition offers a bracing follow up to put uttered vows into real action. The liturgy speaks of the process of *teshuvah*, or repentance, a three-step process of true reconciliation with God. First, one must recognize faults and mistakes. Second, one must vow to make change for the better. And finally, one must be willing to choose differently when the opportunity presents itself to err again. Usually, the moral rubber of repentance rarely hits the road of challenge until weeks or months later. But after an inspired (hopefully) morning of worship and a lunch that can put the heartiest of souls into a full food coma, the ceremony of *tashlich* offers an immediate opportunity to walk the walk that was talked that morning.

Tashlich means casting, and it is a literal throwing of

bread upon the waters, although for a different purpose than classically intended. Many modern Jews are uncomfortable with the literalism of the ritual. Breadcrumbs symbolize our sins, and tossing them overboard is a physical reflection of our longing to rid ourselves of a year's worth of spiritual bloopers, blowups, and breakdowns. Many modern Jews reject this as superstition, the physicalization of a process of repentance that is more dignified as an inner, metaphoric struggle.

A small, manmade water run-off from a larger creek ran near a congregation I served. At the time, my congregation proudly rejected the *tashlich* ritual as a kind of Jew Voodoo. The congregation was on a street dubbed "Rue de la Shul" for its many synagogues. One Rosh Hashanah afternoon I took a contemplative walk around the synagogue property and came to the run-off. I looked into the waters seeking a relaxing, trance-induced state, but the gentle babbling was rudely obscured by loaves of bread littering the flow. Someone or *someones* (I hope) had obviously had a year preferably left in Vegas but unfortunately emblazoned on conscience. I wondered if my neighbors from the nearby Orthodox shul had wandered to an adjacent community for anonymity, or if some amongst my thoroughly modern and rational flock sought to cover their bases by backsliding into the tribal realm of sympathetic magic.

My current congregation is in Seattle, a city anomalous for many reasons. Two of the most obvious: an almost fanatical individualism which defies the impulse to join groups, including houses of worship; and a hyper-sensitivity to the environment growing out of the unimaginable beauty of the region and its attractiveness to outdoor-types who are puritanical in their protective instincts. During our *tashlich* ceremony on Lake Washington, while some resonate with the physicality of throwing bread into the water (which is greedily gobbled up by ducks, geese, and gulls), there is another way to observe the ritual.

The brief liturgy I compiled for this ceremony speaks of the great sins civilization has heaped upon the world in the form of pollution and other byproducts of progress. Rather than contribute to this ongoing crisis, the service inspires people to "take [trash] with us as a sign of our appreciation, a mark of our concern, proof of our changing attitude." In small but significant ways, the process of personal transformation toward effecting change in the broader world, the key dynamic of the High Holiday season, is borne out soon after the morning's worship, making real what could have been mere righteous lip service.

The text from Torah that speaks most meaningfully to the environmental issue comes, not surprisingly, from the first of the five books, the Creation account of Genesis. Its unavoidable presence and power have turned the hearts of even the most selective biblical literalists. There is a growing movement amongst evangelicals for "Creation Care," a long-delayed but much welcomed acknowledgement that genuine fidelity to the words and intent of the Bible demands unequivocal support of conservation and an utter rejection of despoiling nature for corporate convenience. It has caused a schism within the evangelical movement, marginalizing those who have sold their souls for a place at the Conservative trough of corporate largesse, anti-intellectualism, and the all-consuming idolatry of neo-Puritanism.

There are actually two creation stories recounted in Chapter 1 and Chapter 2 of Genesis. Some see the second as a counter-point to ideas that appear in the first story, and some see it as a complement to the previous account. The two stories demonstrate the richness and complexity of the biblical text, whose authors well understood that critical issues are not reckoned in black and white, but require the gray shades of human fallibility, error, and promise. The second account conveys the evolving theology of the biblical authors who transformed folktales of life's beginnings into mythic illustrations of an emerging moral system.

The first creation account is the one more familiar and more often used to justify rapacious exploitation of the earth by those seeking religious justification for concession to greed:

And God blessed them, and God said to them,
Be fruitful, and multiply, and fill the earth, and
subdue it; and have dominion over the fish of the
sea, and over the birds of the air, and over every
living thing that moves upon the earth.

If taken alone as God's sole guidance on the issue of human agency in nature, it would, indeed, provide fairly bleak prospects for striking an integrated balance between human need and the integrity of nature. And taking it merely on its face, without the interpretive struggle and metaphoric intent of the authors, does grave injustice to the text's potential as God's will, a will that continues to be revealed with each successive reading.

While clearly human-centric, written during an ancient period in which people sought not so much mastery but merely some insight into the seemingly capricious power of the elements that both nurtured and destroyed them, it would be delusional to either teach or believe that using resources exhaustively was God's intent. God commanding humankind to be "fruitful and multiply" encourages the kind of rampant propagation people saw in other species. And this first of God's commands (yes, sexual congress is both a divine mandate and first amongst them) responded to the fears of death and extinction that sparked the earliest spiritual yearnings.

The more controversial command verbs are "fill" and "subdue." Again, these are less the marching orders of a haughty, imperial deity than comforting support for those who felt that everything in the world conspired against their survival. It's a kind of overcompensation, as when a football coach inspires a struggling, demoralized team at half-time to face another thirty minutes on the field against a formidable foe. Imagine Pat O'Brian playing God as Knute Rockney (not a great leap for Notre Dame fans) compelling Adam and Eve to "win one for the Gipper," and you get the idea.

As for "dominion," some fundamentalist Christians have created virtually another denomination based on the arrogant and triumphalist fantasies of a Christendom that vanquishes not only unbelievers, but the world itself. The notion of dominion can be unpacked in many ways. One way is to compare the developing view of God amongst the ancient Hebrews to the surrounding cultures at the time.

Many of the Canaanite gods, and the monarchs who claimed descent and divinity from them, were demanding, subjugating tyrants. They exploited and ravaged their people, requiring unquestioning obedience through the blood of babies on bonfires and compulsory prostitution for young women in the pagan temples. One of Judaism's many radical departures from this context was the vision of a God who transcended humanity not just in form, but in sensibilities. The God of Israel did not need the petty offerings and ego-stroking tribute of god-kings and was distinct from the pagan gods imbued with the most shallow of human qualities.

The God of Israel, while determined to establish justice, was compassionate, nurturing, and hopeful for the people. Human beings were no longer objectified as material proof of faith on murderous altars. An incorporeal, all-powerful God did not need to be "fed" through sacrifice. The distinctly Jewish act of offering, of sacrificing something of value, transformed the *people themselves*. Sacrifices did not add anything to a whole, complete, and perfect God. God did not need. God taught the people to give something of material value in order to gain something invaluable, something that would endure for generations.

This model of a wise, caring, and just monarch inspired the kings of Israel, who were beholden to the Law of Israel and were deposed if they abused their power. This pattern of monarchical behavior, in turn, augmented the developing impression of the God of Israel as a ruler whose concern echoed that of a magnanimous sovereign. Thus, when we are commanded by God to exercise dominion over the earth, it is with the expectation that such power will be used judiciously, holistically, and enduringly.

The verse from the second Creation account is both complementary and expository. It's as if the authors needed to further clarify and expound upon the first version, an impulse seen clearly in this addition to the command for human agency in nature:

> *And the Lord God took the man, and put him into the Garden of Eden to cultivate it and to keep/protect it.*

Yes, God expects us to interact with nature, to use our God-given ingenuity and skill to do more than survive, but to thrive and flourish, perhaps even in comfort! The sense of *cultivation* encompasses both a modification of the land for expressed purpose, but also a sustaining of the resource for future use. This expectation is reinforced by the verb paired with the word *cultivate*, the Hebrew *sh-mor*, connoting the diligent observance of a command or the careful protection of a thing or idea.

This verb conveys the dynamic compelling a Jew's observance of the Sabbath, the most central experience binding Israel in covenant to its God. Using it in the context of human responsibility for nature offers a clear intent, urges an unmistakable lesson: the protection of the earth is a key component of the covenant with God, the essence of a Jew's communion with the divine. We are tenants seeking to show respect and appreciation for the generosity of our Ultimate Landlord.

This concept informs a key distinction between Judaism and other faiths. While many faiths are concerned with how actions in this life impact the next, Jews focus on the present. While many pursue the good and avoid evil to secure a place in the world to come, Jews seek ways to make this world the best that it can be. If anything, we are not investors in a future redemption. We are debtors who can never totally repay the kindness and regard reflected in the act of creation. Yet we must never tire of making the effort, of using our precious few years to leave something more than a mere footprint—to leave an impression that enriches rather than consumes, an imprint that inspires the next generation rather than evoking a lament for the passing of the "good old days."

How does this ancient wisdom inform awareness of Spirit at the Center of our being and the action it demands? We can look to another account of creation beyond the biblical text. Kabbalah, the mystical movement in Judaism, was consumed by questions of God's essence and the true nature of Creation. The kabbalistic genesis myth envisions God as engaging in an act of *tzimtzum*, a compression that preceded and enabled the act of creation.

Even God, the Omniscience and the Omnipotence behind time, space, and matter needed to withdraw, to contract, to become *less than* in order to provide the requisite space for the creation of something *other than* God. Before there could be reality and life, God needed to create empty space. While all creation emanated from God, it needed a place to exist apart from God.

In Judaism, God is not only the Ultimate Teacher imparting lessons, God is also the Ultimate Exemplar. We can never be God, but we are commanded by God to imbue our lives with the few divine qualities we can discern in a lifetime. If God possesses the humility and insight to pull back in order to provide the space and resources for life to flourish, should we not strive for a similar restraint?

Our act of *tzimtzum*, of contraction from our ambitions to fill the world with our presence, bend it to our will or conform it to our agenda requires *sacrifice*. We must be willing to give up immediate gratification, a transient sense of imminent accomplishment. We are so consumed with the race to succeed, to grow, to confront, and to conquer, that we obscure the costs of this head-long plunge toward an ever-receding finish line. We forget that there is no true, real success if others are unable to take even the first step in this *human race*. If our pursuits deny our children the chance to experience the journey granted to us, we not only ignore the modeled lesson of an inspiring God, we arrogantly reject the grand intelligence, the sacred scheme that envisions a creation able to sustain itself beyond that first act of blessed intervention.

There are as many ways to offer grateful sacrifice *to* God and *for* God's creation as there are ways to abuse our plenty and deny our potential. Today's environmental movement focuses on fossil fuels as pollutants and as driver of foreign policy adventure and ambition. Tomorrow's concerns and conflicts will grow from resources as elemental as water and air. Better to spark awareness and foster habits of sacrifice now, with something as relatively non-essential as oil-made-energy for our cars, homes, and industries, than to wait to cultivate these critical abilities when the stakes are even higher, the consequences more dire.

In finding a faith basis for environmental awareness and change, this embrace of God as model for Spirit at the Center of our being extends naturally to Spirit at the Center of our ideology. In the most basic calculus of *realpolitik*, the approach of *New York Times* columnist Thomas Friedman and others speaks to the fear rampant in our society today. If our gravest concern is for national security, then the environment must be a priority. No less likely a progressive source than the Pentagon has issued reports that reach this conclusion.

If we truly care about the defense of our nation, if we genuinely seek to marginalize and isolate religious fundamentalists and the regimes that bankroll them, reducing the rush of petrodollars into their coffers is a good place to start. But it requires personal commitment as much as, and perhaps more than, a foreign policy change of course. If we seek to instill in our youth discipline, perspective, and more visionary priority setting, the importance of sacrifice to character development is critical.

This goes against the grain of many who cannot resist giving in to their child's every material demand, let alone their own. In the West in particular, *want* and *have* are separated merely by *the ask*. The same is not true for the vast majority of the world's population. Insulating our young in a cocoon of privilege and excess produces not only a generation of the pampered and the weak, it severs bonds of human kinship and identification with the rest of the world. Those who constantly want are seen to somehow deserve the hand they've been dealt. Those who suffer are amongst fate's inevitable victims. The need to give up something for the greater good and, perhaps most importantly, for an unseen ideal, is as good for the soul as it is for the world. It is as crucial to childrearing as vaccinations, hot food, and a roof over their heads, preferably with cable and WiFi preinstalled.

In the biblical text, when God seeks to reward the Israelites for their fidelity to the commandments, fertility and security were the blessings that most motivated faith to a little known deity and its demands. These were the most basic, urgent needs in the ancient world. And despite our many advances, comforts, and defenses against the short, nasty and brutish existence of our ancestors, family welfare and societal safety still rank high amongst survival's Top Ten. And with a moral symmetry that almost seems *planned*, the commandments that earned this reward had far more to do with reaching out to the needy and establishing a just society than appeasing the caprice of a demanding God.

In essence, God has little to do with the current state of the world. The task and the challenge are ours alone. But God or tradition or the sum of our ethical genius provides a good and right way. Embracing the commandments is its own reward, inevitably leading to personal and national blessing. These priorities are neither politically conservative nor progressive. They are foundational, and they are holy.

Give Shalom a Chance

It's one of my most indelible memories of childhood. I was in 6th grade, standing in the lunch line waiting for my daily dose of the starches, sugars, and fats that passed for nutrition in the world of '70s institutional food preparation. The discussions in line usually ranged from the mundane to the ridiculous: the perfection of Farrah Fawcett's hair while judo flipping thugs on the previous night's *Charlie's Angels*, or the poor performance of the San Francisco Giants throughout the season (and decade during the '70s).

It was unusual for even a spark of the sublime to slip into this junior Algonquin Round Table before reaching the lunch lady's crushing ladle of chicken tetrazzini or beef stroganoff. But for some reason, this day's *tete a tete* ranged beyond Farrah's locks or Bobby Bond's performance. For some reason, we lit upon the subject of Jesus. This was an all boys private school, with a rather significant population of Jews aspiring to plug in to the WASP network of prep schools, ivy league secret societies, and a bloodless life of scotch-soaked desperation. Still, the subject of religion rarely came up, and when it did, it was assumed to be of the generic Protestant variety.

I was the son of a rabbi, so I not only represented all things Jewish to the gentiles and Jews passing as gentiles, I felt I harbored a secret, esoteric insight into *"the way things really are"*—the truth beyond the misapprehension of common knowledge. I don't know what possessed me that noontime. Maybe it was the overpowering need to finally assert my minority identity, emboldened by the intoxicating fumes of processed cheese sauce and mildewing cafeteria mop. I blurted out, perhaps in a way not even germane to the content or rhythm of the conversation: "Ya know, Jesus was a Jew."

While Albert Schweitzer had asserted this concept seven decades earlier in his exploration of the historical Jesus, cutting-edge Christian scholarship had embraced this as a given, and the Second Vatican Council had been safely ensconced in the cultural consciousness for more than ten years, the word seemed not to have trickled down to the privileged enclaves of San Francisco's Pacific Heights.

I met blank stares and slack jaws that soon grew into furrowed brows, pursed lips, and if I had bothered to look down, probably clenched fists. The words struck me full force in my clueless naiveté: "If you say that again, I'm gonna punch you in the face." How could my words have been so misunderstood, my intention so misinterpreted? Didn't everyone seek the same fact, the same insight, the same truth as I? Part of me felt slighted at this affront to my good intentions. But with some time and perspective, even as a middle-schooler lacking in life experience and broader study, I began to appreciate the nerve I had struck, the world-view I had challenged, and the faith I had threatened.

The late Israeli Prime Minister Yitzhak Rabin, assassinated in 1995 by a Jewish extremist who sought to end Israel's peace initiatives by ending Rabin's heart beat, saw the enemy clearly. After years of fighting Arab nations and Palestinian terrorists, he came to a late-in-life epiphany that the greatest challenge to wellbeing and security was fundamentalism, regardless of its faith origins. His words prophetically foretold his fate.

The post 9/11 world has revealed the evil designs and realizations of Islamic religious fundamentalism. But the Western response poses a similarly dire threat to our righteous sense of national self. In our defense, we lower thresholds for armed conflict, demonize entire cultures as faceless enemies, and flog fear as justification to suspend the legal and moral structure unique to our democratic identity. Despite our less nefarious intentions in relation to Islamic zealotry, it is a painful irony that, in many ways, we are on the road to becoming the ideological mirror image of those we seek to destroy.

Though our nation remains a stalwart refuge of tolerance and opportunity, we risk losing our national soul in the ways we confront growing global fanaticism.

Terrorism is the tool of absolutist ideologies that seek to bring the world down to their level of dualistic morality and theological certainty. The aspiration of righteous nations is to combat these ideas and acts with a measured, defensive response and to resist giving in to the fears and insecurities that compel the fundamentalist. The ultimate weapon in our arsenal is the ability to live well and stay good, to remain a shining beacon to an uncertain world, especially in the face of crisis, tragedy, and fear.

Remaining true to our core beliefs requires constant scrutiny and honest self-assessment. Spirit at the Center of being and ideology stands as a potent point of reference against which we can gauge how far we've strayed from that core, helping us chart the way back to who we really are and who we long to be.

The biblical text asserts early on how diversity is a critical component of the human condition, and how acceptance of variation is necessary for a stable, enduring civilization. The 11th chapter of Genesis culminates the Bible's myth of human origins before the next chapter narrows into the specific story of the Jewish people. The conclusion of the chapter contains a terse, frequently misinterpreted passage. It is a story we learn as children, but often never encounter again through the prism of adult apprehension and the subtler insights that can only be gleaned through more years and life experience.

At its most basic level, the Tower of Babel passage is merely etiological, a common inspiration for myth as explanation for why things are the way they are now. It filled the credulity gap between the Creation story of common ancestry and the real world experience of a multitude of languages and cultures. It is a fable of simple cause and effect: arrogant humanity sought to build a pathway to God, and God humbled these high flyers by "babeling" their tongues—literally confusing their languages so they could not complete their grandiose effort.

Despite its economy of language, the text reveals an interaction between God and humanity of greater nuance and meaning. We revealingly peer into the consciousness and concerns of the people

And they said, Come, let us build us a city and
a tower, whose top may reach to heaven; and let
us make us a name, lest we be scattered abroad
upon the face of the whole earth.

In these few words, when read with more care and empathy, we see that the people are not pursuing self-aggrandizement as much as responding to fear of being alone and forgotten. In seeking a *name*, they aren't merely angling for a Warholian moment in the klieg lights or striving to become the You Tube flavor of the month. They long for something more essential and existential: a place in the memory of future generations, the hope that their brief sojourn will leave a mark more enduring than the crumbling ruins of even the greatest empires of the past. They seek not to *become God* through the height of a Tower reaching toward the heavens, but to bind together through common cause against the isolation of a nomadic life in the wilderness. These basic and urgent human needs, a supportive community, and a sense that death does not snuff out all evidence of our existence, are perhaps the most compelling forces driving the development of religion in human history.

God's response is also deeper than what is discerned in a first pass over the text:

And the Lord said, Behold, the people are one, and they have all one language; and this they begin to do; and now nothing will be restrained from them, which they have schemed to do. Come, let us go down, and there confuse their language, that they may not understand one another's speech. So the Lord scattered them

abroad from there upon the face of all the earth;
and they left off the building of the city.

It is easy, perhaps too easy, to ascribe the identifiable and anthropomorphic notion that God's ego is threatened. And it's a fragile ego at that! God seems petty, merely wanting to prevent humanity from gaining the power to challenge God on the "home court" of the heavens. The response seems like a justified punishment from a punitive parent for childish foibles and delusions of grandeur.

But perhaps a better explanation lies in a passage we studied earlier. Again, the first command to humanity in the Creation story after existence has been established dictates

Be fruitful, and multiply, and fill the earth...

The third clause bears profoundly on the Babel story. God commands humanity to populate the earth not only quantitatively, but qualitatively—to spread over the earth, to create cultures and communities in all places, to utilize the great possibilities of the planet to the fullest extent possible.

God's command, though compelling, is often obscured by the overpowering call of human insecurity.

The people seek strength and courage from staying together. But God envisions another way. The scattering of humanity is the fulfillment of God's original command and intent. This is so fundamental a process that we see it in nature, as when the adult bird scoots the reticent chick out of the nest, or retirees depleting their 401Ks suggest to their 26-year-old grad student that the time has come to leave the basement and find a roommate. God engages in a bit of "tough love," doing what is best for the children, empowering them to become self-sufficient whether they feel they are ready or not.

What is most interesting is the manner in which God implements this goal. For humanity to fulfill its potential for growth, to maximize the bounty of the earth and to embrace the natural course synonymous with God's will, humanity is distinguished through a diversity of languages and cultures. The differences that seem to so often divide us are actually necessary for us to become fully human, fully realized according to God's vision for the ongoing, unfolding act of creation.

We often respond to difference with fear, acting out against the unknown or little known *other* with bigotry and violence. But this response is like the building of the Tower, another example of how frailty and insecurity blot out an appreciation for God's intent. Thus, just as God's scattering rectified the Tower's deviation from the right path, so too must we embrace a divine perspective, implementing the divine gifts of wisdom and compassion to overcome suspicion of difference, fear, and hatred of the Other.

The Tower of Babel story, like the Bible at its best, is an accessible metaphor inspiring us to realize the seemingly unachievable and the unprecedented. God's direct intercession at Babel symbolizes the way we must be open to God working indirectly through us. Or in a broader, non-theistic sense, the story symbolizes the openness needed to accept many different "others" toward achieving a common good. With a growing appreciation that diversity is the goal, the plan, and the purpose, our choice is whether to thwart or bring about this ideal in the world. This awareness is the Spirit at the Center of our being, a sacred prism through which we see the world and determine our place in it. But we must also be willing to act on that awareness, forging revealed insight into a change of heart that inspires the work of hands. The principles of pluralism and *shalom* reflect just such a Spirit at the Center of ideology, the blueprint for a course of action.

The modern Orthodox rabbi and maverick communal leader, Yitz Greenberg, teaches that one of the highest ideals to which we should aspire is pluralism. He describes it as a "unity without uniformity." For Greenberg, there is a consensus that emerges from a genuine respect for others, an appreciation for the regard with which they cherish their traditions. But this respect and appreciation does not diminish the integrity of our traditions or their priority in our lives. An authentic pluralism does not obligate us to believe that all paths to God or truth or right are correct—just that they are valid and important.

Both Rabin and Greenberg speak to the conflict that has marred human history and threatens the stability of the world today. Religious fanaticism, ideological fundamentalism, and xenophobic nationalism are at the blackened heart of what ails the human spirit and what imperils us all. A pluralistic approach that expands our passions and sense of purpose to encompass a respect for what moves and inspires others enables all of us to live and flourish in a diverse, dynamic world.

This is more than the celebrated value of "tolerance," which is, in the words of our 43rd President, a "bigotry of low expectations." We're not asking much when we expect tolerance—the ability to *put up* with others. It is not a far descent down the ladder of human interaction from tolerance to intolerance, from *putting up* with someone to *putting them out*. Pluralism challenges us at the core, compelling us to empathize with another, to reach into the heart and conscience of another, to imagine ourselves as the other. Mere toleration does little to effect change. Mere toleration underestimates and undervalues our capacity for change.

Pluralism is not a blanket acceptance of all attitudes and actions. There is a perverse faith that denies the rights of others, even the right to existence. There is a skewed pursuit of perceived good that most of us justly regard as evil. Pluralism is not the situational ethics of acceptance of all difference. There are universal truths and a consensus of behavior that affirm our ability to live together. The imposition of one belief system on others is anathema. Violent and murderous implementation of one worldview on others is an unequivocal wrong. We may debate the finer points of difference, but we must agree that security of our person and respect for boundaries are necessary for a civilization to exist that can even hope to embrace pluralism. Pluralism is not a suicide pact, nor a pursuit of mutually assured destruction.

The concept that encompasses both a rejection of fundamentalism and an embrace of pluralism is *shalom*. Shalom is more than a Hebrew version of the multi-purpose Hawaiian greeting *aloha*. It is commonly understood as *peace*, as the absence of conflict. And while it encompasses an anti-war sentiment, it means much more. Understanding and embracing the deeper, transcendent levels of *shalom* has the potential to salve the spiritual wounds for which violence, bigotry, and hatred are but symptoms.

The true origins of the word shalom are rooted in the Hebrew root meaning *wholeness* or *completion*. Israeli friends routinely greet one another with *ma sh-lom-cha*—idiomatically translated as "How are you?" but literally connoting a sense of "How is your state of wholeness?" In the Jewish prayerbook, we pray that God grants blessings of peace "at every moment and every hour *bishlomecha*—with Your [God's] complete being." The modern Hebrew word for paying money is *l'shalem*, conveying a sense of making another financially whole.

There are concentric circles of shalom that determine our spiritual well being, and thus our ability to work for the welfare of the world. We must first find a *shalom of self.* Before we can effect change beyond, we must struggle for change within. As a remedy for the narrowness of spirit afflicting the fundamentalist, shalom of self is potent.

The key crisis for the fundamentalist is insecurity driven by fear: fear of modernity, fear of change, and fear of the unknown that implants uncertainty regarding the purpose of life, its values and priorities. The only way to overcome this fear is through a confrontation with the darker parts of the self. It is a transformative struggle that often emerges from crisis.

There are two paths we can take at the crossroads of crisis. We can impulsively fight what we fear, lashing out in a desperate attempt to ward off or destroy a perceived threat. This is the path of fundamentalism. We condemn, attack, and kill, a delusional quest to control a world that whizzes by as we stand firm in myopic, futile obstinacy. We seek security in an imagined past, a hearkening back to periods of primitivism and ignorance that bring comfort simply because they are known, not because they are better. It is an increasingly impossible and dangerous reaction to an ever-moving, ever-shrinking world.

The other path entails using crisis constructively. It requires a radical rebuilding of the self, emerging from a breaking down of something within us. This process is not confined to humanity. Rather, it reflects the cycles of nature of which we are an integral part—the cycle in which death and decay produces new life and new purpose. The biblical story of Jacob is apt metaphor for facing a moment of crisis and using it to embrace a constructive breaking down toward a changed self rather than provoking a destructive annihilation of a feared other.

Throughout his life, Jacob endured great success and abject failure. He strove toward his revealed destiny through acts of courage and principle. And he descended into dark solitude, the just desserts of a deceit that enabled his rise and would continue to be visited upon him. On a material level, he was a man of power and possessions as he approached midlife. Yet he still had not attained his full potential as a person, or earned the mantle of tribal patriarch in covenant with God. In his youthful petulance, naked ambition consumed patience and perspective, as family intrigue entwined with prophecy and bad parenting to shatter bonds seemingly beyond repair.

After years of alienation, Jacob gets word that his brother Esau seeks a meeting. Jacob learns that Esau comes with a retinue of family and tribesman, and he imagines that Esau is preparing to settle old accounts. But the stakes are now higher, as Jacob has far more to lose in life and kin. Still viewing the world through the petty prism of agenda and ego, Jacob projects his own anger and jealousy onto a vision of Esau's vengeful state of mind.

Jacob leaves his family on one bank of the river Jabbok and remains on the other side to endure what St. John of the Cross would later characterize as a "dark night of the soul." At this highly symbolic and liminal spot, the classic, mythic boundary between the physical and the spiritual, Jacob battles a mysterious figure. Is it an angel, or Esau himself sneaking into the camp, or a metaphoric account of inner turmoil? Clerics, shrinks, and charlatans have filled the interpretive ambiguity with self-justifying exegesis. What is most critical is the aftermath of the encounter.

Jacob emerges from the struggle forever changed, humbled but wiser, limping but finally empowered to walk his appointed path. The wound from this melee is a bodily reminder of his transformation, something to take forward when apathy and complacency threaten to dull the lessons of the past. He receives a blessing from his adversary in the form of a name: He is now called "Yisrael," which means one who has struggled with divinity.

The next day, Jacob goes out to meet his brother and his fate without the fear of the previous day. He is a different person, with a new clarity of self and purpose. He need not worry about the threats that Jacob faced. Yisrael is a new man with a clean slate awaiting the inscriptions of infinite possibility. Yisrael is released from the pettiness and grudges of his primitive, personal history. He is reborn, resigned in blissful submission to God's plan and providence.

Immediately, Esau perceives and appreciates the metamorphosis. The years of strife and resentment melt into a sobbing embrace of what was lost and what is left to share. There can be reconciliation with Esau only when Jacob's change is evident, when Jacob's weariness and woundedness supplant memories of the haughty youth of a troubled past. And Jacob cannot ascend into his rightful role as leader of a people, as agent of God's will and vision, until he is reconciled with those he hurt, until he is unburdened of such devastating failures of self. In this moment, personal growth and realized destiny synthesize into something greater than their separate strands.

There is a sacred, spiritual symbiosis that renders Jacob/ Yisrael worthy of eponymous descendents.

Jacob's embrace of crisis, the needed tearing down and recreation of the self, the transformation that empowered his broader capacity to transform others and the world, is a potent model for the shalom of self that is necessary for any larger movement or ideology. Unless we are reconciled to ourselves, how can we reach out authentically to those closest to us? And unless we foster healthy, functional relationships with our most intimate others, how can we hope to contribute to a larger, global redemption?

The second concentric circle of shalom is, of course, built on the first. When we recognize, appreciate, and strive to achieve that which brings us wholeness and wellbeing, we better understand what we must secure for others. Western efforts to export "civilization" in past centuries and "democracy" today reflect not merely a lack of empathy for other cultures, but a willful ignorance of the most basic needs and aspirations of others.

While I disagree with many of Thomas Friedman's theories regarding "globalism" as the panacea for the world's ills, he is correct in asserting economic deprivation as a key motivation for fundamentalism. A young man with steady income and prospects for the future is less likely to strap on explosives and take out a Tel Aviv food court than a desperate, hopeless resident of a squalid refugee camp. There will always be extremists who drink the Koolaid and kill the innocent out of a perverse conviction promulgated by and skewed through the delusional egos of petty mullahs and tin-badge dictators. But the marginal and fanatical will have a shrinking pool of canon fodder for the evil they are too cowardly to execute themselves if the street offers a hope the heart can embrace.

The confidence in a purposeful present and the vision for a promising future can transcend even the most contentious of perennial feuds. And while economic prosperity and security do not fulfill all needs, when they are lacking they consume all possibility. There can be no empathy for another's dreams when our children go hungry. There can be no reaching toward a different world when the weight of the world-as-it-is is borne in despair. Our basic comfort and the broader dignity of others, the viability of our dreams and empathy for those of another are inextricably bound and mutual. In our best moments, we long to obtain for others the basics we insist upon for ourselves. But we can only reach beyond the self from a secure self. This is the only foundation upon which higher ideals, lofty visions and true pluralism can be built.

The third circle of shalom grows from our relationship with God. Again, as encouraged throughout this book, God transcends the classic, personal, and anthropomorphic sense that alienates many. A wholeness of self that breeds confidence, security, and hope, and a moral obligation to support the welfare, dignity, and dreams of others are both reflections of a singular, unified power, purpose, and force in the universe that supports life and rejects what endangers, diminishes, or obscures life. Is that Unified Power an idealized image of a unity we seek in the world? Or are our ideals inspired by what we know of God? This is a question for theologians, philosophers, and the pungent, smoke-filled rooms of late-night college dormitories. If we seek a positive, life-affirming goal, it matters little whether its pursuit is the product of human moral evolution or divine revelation. If a recognition of this Great Oneness helps to convince others of our common humanity, if we can learn to recognize a spark of the One in All and revere and cherish the person who houses the spark, we are closer to what faith deems "the messianic time," what philosophy regards as "utopia," and what each of us knows, perhaps at an unconscious, molecular level, as "the way things are meant to be."

Starting with regard for self, moving to embrace the needs of others, and finally encompassing God in this matrix of relationships and realizations, we imbue ideology with a spiritual value beyond the religious chauvinism and narrowness that has produced fear, discord, and violence throughout our history. How remarkable, dare I say even *miraculous*, that we transient creatures in a vast universe possess the capacity, through a change in awareness and a commitment to act on that experience, to profoundly alter our reality. It is an act worthy of God.

And in the End...

PRESIDENTIAL CANDIDATES OFTEN DON THE MANTLE OF LAUDED LEADERS FROM AN IMAGINED PAST. The recent horse race to the White House offered its own quirky forays into this acquisition of road-tested identity. John F. Kennedy has been a go-to archetype for aspirants seeking the label of the young, idealistic maverick who rises above the conventions and constraints of the past, the one who will chart a course toward a "New Frontier."

Aside from Kennedy's vanguard ideas and obvious youth, as the first Catholic to run for President, his candidacy challenged civic assumptions, most of them prejudicial, about the interplay between faith and politics and the influence of personal belief upon official policy. Kennedy decided to confront these concerns directly in a famous address before his clerical and ideological critics. Kennedy's courage and conviction swayed many fence-sitters and those who never imagined they would vote for someone possessing *exotic* origins beyond the cozy comfort zone of WASPdom.

With Kennedy's success in mind, 2008 Republican Presidential primary contender Mitt Romney hoped that a 40 year-old breakthrough for Catholics might resonate down through the decades to work its magic for the nation's first Mormon candidate. But the Kennedy mojo did little to charge a speech that hardly addressed Mormon doctrine, but rather laid out a perversion of the church/state dynamic that Kennedy had so artfully envisioned. And worse, Romney's true confessions further shored up the battle lines between those for whom belief is integral to citizenship and those who see the two as necessarily distinct in a healthy republic.

Conservative columnist David Brooks, while respectful, summed up the larger concerns emerging from Romney's message.

> *When this country was founded, James Madison envisioned a noisy public square with different religious denominations arguing, competing and balancing each other's passions. But now the landscape of religious life has changed. Now its most prominent feature is the supposed war between the faithful and the faithless. Mitt*

Romney didn't start this war, but speeches like his both exploit and solidify this divide in people's minds.

Brooks' *New York Times* colleague on the left, Roger Cohen, leveled a similar critique, though from more anticipated quarters. Cohen's fears stem from Romney's increasing reliance on personal faith as a basis for civic leadership, a mash-up of ideological realms that the Founders expressly sought to avoid, a theocratic worldview aptly reflected by our greatest foe in this "clash of civilizations."

Such beliefs [that political leadership is divinely guided] seem to remove decision-making from the realm of the rational at the very moment when the West's enemy acts in the name of fanatical theocracy. At worst, they produce references to a "crusade" against those jihadist enemies. God-given knowledge is scarcely amenable to oversight...Where Kennedy said he believed in a "president whose religious views are his own private affair," Romney pledged not to "separate us from our religious heritage.".... Religion informed America's birth. But its distancing from politics was decisive to the republic's success. Indeed, the devastating European experience of religious war influenced the founders' thinking. That is why I find Romney's speech and the society it reflects far more troubling than Europe's vacant cathedrals.

Coming from both ends of the ideological spectrum, this brace of indictments against Romney's views of faith and politics is a hopeful sign that the warring camps of religion and reason are finding common ground while relegating their extremists to the margins of civil society.

Perhaps one of the most disturbing sound bites from Romney's manifesto was the rhetorically symmetrical but philosophically baseless notion that "Freedom requires religion just as religion requires freedom." Well, he's partially right...the part that is affirmed in the First Amendment's assurance of the free exercise of religion. Any practice of faith beyond a tyrannical theocracy indeed requires freedom, but the converse is not true, as Cohen wryly counters, "...secular Sweden is free while religious Iran is not." While Romney may be politically adroit in his word-play, if he truly buys into this obvious pandering to the conservative base, his presidency would represent a radical departure from two-and-a-half centuries of refined balance between the law of the soul and the soul of law.

And genuine freedom and delicate balance are so desperately needed in these passion-filled times. It's what lies at the heart of a Spirit at the Center: Finding that balance between faith in a greater power and faith in the power of people, between the call of conscience and the obligations of civil society. Our personal freedom to believe or not, to seek transcendence or not, to imbue our lives with holiness or not, is an unalienable right, if not imbued by God, then certainly guaranteed by virtue of our membership in the human race.

Faith is not the sole foundation for the pursuit of good in the world. While inspiring and motivating for many, unequivocal belief in God and adherence to formal religion is but one pathway to forging and sustaining the kind of world in which all can enjoy life, liberty, and the pursuit of happiness. Protecting a society in which private beliefs are insulated from public pressures and public policy shielded from private agendas is a distinguishing American virtue. Safeguarding personal freedoms while providing a safe place for public expression and consensus is the foundation of democracy.

There are other recent encouraging signs of both moderation from the ideological extremes and an emerging critique from the growing center. From the infamous Evangelical Right, a seeming invulnerable juggernaut after the 2004 Presidential elections, the Holy Trinity of God, Gays, and Guns has given way to more global, universal concerns. Chastened by their electoral rebuke in the 2006 congressional vote, the religious right has come to Jesus in new and constructive ways that more aptly reflect the essential message of the Nazarene carpenter.

A schism cleaves the old school Jerry Falwell/Pat Robertson brand of pop puritanism from a new generation of preachers and believers. The New Evangelicals appreciate pressing human need beyond an obsession with fetal development, determining the gender of applicants for marriage licenses, and enshrining the right to publicly praise Jesus before the West Texas high school football championship game.

Journalist David Kirkpatrick traced this evolution, noting changes emerging from economic and theological growth. Evangelicals have moved from the rural exurbs to the middle-class suburbs. Geographic change brings with it different priorities and concerns, as higher levels of education and awareness open up the challenges of a wider world beyond one's own experience. There is a newly discovered embrace of the *other* that extends beyond the call to share "good news," a more compelling need to secure the welfare of the body and dignity of the person over a patronizing regard for the state of the un-saved soul.

Theologically, the pessimistic view that the world-as-it-is is a degraded antechamber to the glories of the world-to-come have given way to a sense of hope and obligation to attain the world-that-can-be—to be part of a resolution, even a revolution, inspired both by human need and divine expectation. For these neo-evangelicals, acceptance of Jesus is just the beginning of a personal spiritual formation that will implement Jesus' teachings and example as salve to heal an imperfect world. This vision encompasses both giving to traditional charities and influencing public policy to tackle the daunting global is-sues that have been neglected on the Christian Coalition's legislative agenda.

Pastor Bill Hybels of the archetypal Willowcreek mega-church leads this movement to impart the Bible's more authentic message.

We have just pounded the drum again and again that, for churches to reach their full re-

demptive potential, they have to do more than hold services—they have to try to transform their communities...The Indians are saying to the chiefs, 'We are interested in more than your two or three issues,'...We are interested in the poor, in racial reconciliation, in global poverty and AIDS, in the plight of women in the developing world.

Amongst the issues embraced by this new movement, perhaps the environment is the most controversial driver of the evangelical schism. It threatens to rend apart the well-crafted Republican coalition of social conservatives and supporters of unrestrained, free market capitalism and corporate largesse. And it imbues the physical state of the world with an urgency that those who are counting down to the apocalypse often write off as moot.

The Creation Covenant, signed by many up-and-coming evangelical pastors and theologians, is the manifesto of the Creation Care movement. Rejecting the previous generation's reliance upon scriptural justifications for human *dominion* over the earth to support corporate abuse, advocates of Creation Care see politics not as an end in itself but as a means to achieving real change beyond any one election cycle. They focus more on the Genesis text that places humanity on earth to "till and tend" it. In this way, the earth does not exist merely as horn of plenty to serve human whim. Rather, God commands us to see ourselves as part of a larger whole, to integrate into that whole, and to strive with the whole to achieve the well being of the whole. We are imbued with sacred responsibility as intelligent, morally aware beings to secure this vulnerable, tenuous, and precious gift, if not merely for our own benefit, than as tribute to a generous God.

In the Statement of the Evangelical Climate Initiative, mega-church pastor Rick Warren and many other notable leaders set a new tone and forged a new set of priorities.

We are proud of the evangelical community's long-standing commitment to the sanctity of human life. But we also offer moral witness in many venues and on many issues...While individuals and organizations can be called to concentrate on certain issues, we are not a single-issue movement...Over the last several years many of us have engaged in study, reflection, and prayer related to the issue of climate change...For most of us, until recently this has not been treated as

*a pressing issue or major priority...But now we
have seen and heard enough to offer the following moral argument related to the matter of hu-
man-induced climate change. We commend the
four simple but urgent claims offered in this doc-
ument to all who will listen, beginning with our
brothers and sisters in the Christian community,
and urge all to take the appropriate actions that
follow from them.*

From the other side of the faith debate, there are also
encouraging signs of moderation and unity, a critique of
extremes that seeks to bring all of us together in concerted
effort through common purpose. While the three horse-
men of the new atheist militancy (Harris, Dawkins, and
Hitchens) seem to ride a wave of countercultural contempt, the forces of nuance and sophistication are rising
to confront this myopia from the left—a godless striden-
cy seemingly ignorant of the irony inherent in an attack
on faith that mirrors the fanaticism they decry. Leon
Wieseltier summed up the philosophically shallow and
psychologically telling approach of the new atheists.

*I am increasingly struck by the extent to which
many of the books against God are mainly psy-*

chological expressions. More specifically, a lot of atheism looks to me like just a lot of adolescence. They are always telling you about their parents. They rebel against the false idea that God is the father because they have the false idea that their father is God....When it comes to the articulation of one's view of the world, of one's understanding of what is true and false about the universe, who cares what one's parents believe? The answer is, children care; and there is something childish about the freethinker's pouting critique of his own childhood. Atheism can be as infantilizing as theism, an inverted form of captivity to one's origins, as if biological authority confers intellectual authority...In matters of conviction, we are orphans....Religion may confer a preposterous cosmic significance upon the individual, but atheism is the true friend of egotism.

The growing chorus against the trio of secular inquisitors reveals these mandarins of an imagined Enlightenment renaissance to be far more intellectually reactionary than they purport themselves to be. Author Damon Linker argues that American liberals who root their rejection of ecclesiastical authority in the virtues of antiquity, and find in the Truculent Triplets both kindred spirits and courageous models, should look elsewhere.

...the intellectual lineage to which these authors belong should in fact give liberals pause. Among other problems, it isn't a liberal tradition at all... Many of the Founding Fathers subscribed to deism...And they marked a path that American critics of religion would take again and again: denouncing the foolishness of this or that religious institution while simultaneously affirming one of several heterodox forms of religious belief...In nearly all cases, the form of belief...has been perfectly compatible with liberal government... Rather than seeking common ground with believers as a prelude to posing skeptical questions, today's atheists prefer to skip right to the refutation...It is with this enmity, this furious certainty, that our ideological atheists lapse most fully into illiberalism...modern liberalism derives, at its deepest level, from ancient liberalism—from the classical virtue of liberality, which meant generosity and openness. To be liberal in the classical sense is to accept intellectual variety—and the

*social complexity that goes with it—as the in-
eradicable condition of a free society.*

It is heartening to see the extremes of uncritical faith
and unqualified atheism revealed and reviled for what
they truly are: irrelevant to the majority of us and imper-
iling of a healthy public square. There is a silent majority of the moderate middle that is skeptical of religious
certainty but seeking of spiritual direction. It is a growing community that tires of the one-dimensional battles
from the monomaniacal margins that feed the 24/7 media beast while obscuring the serious search for meaning through joint purpose and common cause. It is for
them—for all of us—that I have laid out this vision. It is
the beginning of a dialogue that, I pray, will continue and
flourish. It is for those who find the demanding journey
more satisfying than the delusion of a certain destination; those whose questions provoke more than forced,
simplistic answers; those who are content with a lack
of the definitive as an essential element of the probing,
striving, sacred human condition. This brief proposal is
dedicated to you.

Spirit at the Center is not a self-help panacea or a
guru's grandiloquent pronouncement. In a world of in-

stant abs and pill-shaped personality change, this can be frustrating. But for most of us, if we look a bit deeper at our longings and our sense of self in the world, we embrace the considered effort required of any worthwhile endeavor. And when the goal is the crafting of a better self toward the creating of a better world, patience and persistence are necessary.

Spirit at the Center is a suggested path for the faithful and the questioning. It is a framework for finding holiness without dogma or doctrine, for seeking the Ultimate Source of all without the constraints of authority or esoterica, for pursuing the good and resisting the darkness without fear or guilt or inadequacy. It is the way of the middle, lacking the exotic, headline-grabbing allure of the radical fringe, but possessing the transcendent, enduring lessons of moderation and equanimity that the greatest minds and most vaulted spirits of the ages have held forth as the key to a long, purposeful life. It is a release of surety for an embrace of opportunity, a relinquishing of security for a seizing of possibility.

I come to this end hoping that this will be the beginning for many. The writing itself has been part challenge, ample exercise, and soul-satisfying confession. Though I live, breathe, and work in the realm of the established religious community, I recognize the more amorphous but no less genuine spiritual longings of so many. My own spirituality tends to exceed the bounds of the faith tradition I teach and sustain. At times, I feel that what I profess professionally varies from what I believe personally. But that is fodder for another written confessional.

I close with the words of two great expositors of modern thought and culture, separated by four centuries of time and light years of experience. Baruch Spinoza's work ushered in modernity's challenge to religious authority, threatening the faithful to the point that reciprocal threats to his life were the only conceivable response for those whose stranglehold on promulgations of truth was slowly but surely being pried away. Spinoza was demonized as a heretic, a murderer of God, and a denier of scriptural truth. With equal hyperbole, he is lauded as the godfather of Enlightenment thought, an unparalleled critic of clergy, and the great liberator of a civilization enslaved in abject servitude to the irrational, the magical, and the fantastic.

As always, the truth lies somewhere in between his characterizations as dragon and St. George. Though courageous in his unprecedented attack on formal religion and its supplanting with reason, there is a subtle irony in his lauding of rationalism to the point of deification. For while Spinoza condemned the abuses and superstition of the priesthood, he found another kind of divinity palpably present in the world and ensconced within the human heart. The complexity and paradoxical nature of Spinoza's system is as much reflection of the authentic, nuanced human experience as it is instructive for those who seek confirmation of their own inspired doubts. The path toward God, or the path of the spirit, or merely the sincere contemplation of things that might be—that should be—is a far worthier pursuit than even the certainty of God's existence

> The highest virtue of the mind is to know God...This virtue is greater the more the mind knows things by this kind of knowledge, and therefore he who knows things by this kind of knowledge passes to the highest human perfection...we clearly understand that our salvation, or blessedness, or liberty consists in a constant and eternal love towards God, or in the love of God towards men. This love or blessedness is called Glory in the sacred writings, and not without reason. For whether it be related to God or to the mind,

*it may properly be called repose of the mind,
which is, in truth, not distinguished from
glory. For in so far as it is related to God, it is
joy...accompanied with the idea of Himself,
and it is the same thing when it is related to
the mind.*

And from the clearly sublime to the unexpectedly so, I conclude with the pinnacle of pop culture, words and music that transcend Top 40 trends and the shallow posturing of pin-ups of the moment. The Beatles brought with them from England more than style and star-power. They conveyed enduring sentiments tersely wedged within the iconic strictures of a three-minute segment of vinyl disc. Though often reduced to a role as the more pop-minded partner to John Lennon's social commentary, Paul McCartney often crafted life lessons that belied the simplistic demands of his chosen genre. At the conclusion of one of the Beatle's last albums, *Abbey Road*, McCartney croons verse that is at once memorable denouement of a definitive work and brilliant sum of the human condition.

*And in the end, the love you take is equal to the
love you make.*

Within these few words, possessing an economy of language to encompass thought that rivals biblical meter, there is a reciprocity of relationship and striving for wholeness that lights the path of personal transformation, expresses our longing to be there for another as we reach for another, and affirms our endless search for the Ultimate Other. It is a quest that begins within the self and continues indefinitely, bounded only by the farthest reaches of the imagination, the inspired dreams of the spirit, and the plumbless depths of the heart.